THE POCKET GUIDE TO
SHOREBIRDS
OF THE
NORTHERN HEMISPHERE

THE POCKET GUIDE TO
SHOREBIRDS
OF THE
NORTHERN
HEMISPHERE

Alan Richards

DRAGON'S WORLD

Dragon's World Ltd.
Limpsfield
Surrey RH8 0DY
Great Britain

First published by Dragon's World 1989

© Dragon's World 1989

© Text and selection of photographs Alan Richards 1989
Copyright in the photographs remains the property of the
individual photographers

British Library Cataloguing in Publication Data

Richards, Alan *1933 –*
    The pocket guide to shorebirds.
    1. Northern hemisphere. Shorebirds
    I. Title
    598'.33

ISBN 1 85028 075 4

Series design by David Allen
Typeset by Action Typesetting Limi   ɔucester
Printed in Singapore

Contents

Introduction

Among the world's approximately 8500 species of birds, there are
some 202 that are generally called 'waders' by European
birdwatchers ('shorebirds' by Americans). Most of these birds are
placed in two families, namely the Sandpipers (Scolopacidae), 85
species, and the Plovers (Charadriidae), 62 species. Additionally,
the Oystercatchers (Haematopodidae) six species, Avocets and Stilts
(Recurvirostridae), six species, and Stone Curlews (Burhinidae),
nine species, are also readily recognized as belonging within this
group. However, the terminology also includes the Lilytrotters

(Jacanidae), seven species, Painted Snipe (Rostratulidae), two species, Coursers and Pratincoles (Glareolidae), 17 species, the Crab Plover (Dromididae), one species, the Ibisbill (Ibidorhynchidae), one species, Seed Snipes (Thincoridae), four species and the Sheathbills (Chionidae), two species.

The majority of these latter mentioned familes are not ostensibly shorebirds, nor do they spend much of their lives wading; nevertheless, all these 12 families belong to the sub-order Charadrii of the order Charadriiformes (which additionally embraces the gulls, the terns and the auks). This book, however, does not set out to cover all the Charadrii worldwide, but concentrates only on

Hilbre Island, Dee Estuary **Overleaf**: City wader roost

those species in the first five families just mentioned that breed in Northern Europe (Western Palearctic). In all, 45 species are dealt with in detail. Europe and North America share many of the same species of shorebirds, either as breeding species or as visitors, and these vagrant species are also dealt with in this book.

Waders are undoubtedly some of the most interesting of the world's birds and also some of the greatest avian travellers, their migrations spanning the globe. In addition, they have great diversity of plumage, many showing complete changes of appearance from summer to winter. Their manner of feeding varies enormously, while their displays and courtship involve some of the

Mixed flock of waders at Hilbre Island including Sanderling, Dunlin and Turnstone

most amazing demonstrations of flight and vocalization to be found within any bird group.

   Though we call these birds waders or shorebirds, it is only for part of their lives that they actually live up to either of these terms. In the breeding season many species nest miles from the sea, some on barren tundras, others in muskeg swamps, others on prairie lands, and a few in arid situations. If any generality of existence can be ascribed to them for all times of the year, it is as birds of open spaces (except perhaps for the Woodcock). It is certainly during the winter months that they more noticeably live up to their name of waders, for it is then they wade most and are mainly to be found on the coast, haunting mudflats, estuaries and marshes, where they often form huge concentrations, their daily routine dictated by the

rise and fall of the tides. It is in such a setting that most observers are familiar with these birds, and we probably know more about their lives for this part of the year. Even today, we have scant knowledge of the breeding biology of a number of species.

It is perhaps due to these birds' association with wetlands that the European expression 'wader' has come about (though in the United States this term is applied to such birds as herons, storks and ibises). In Britain our knowledge of these birds has been greatly added to in recent times through the establishment of the Wader Study Group, the birds and estuaries inquiry initiated by the British Trust for Ornithology, and through the work of many others, particularly ringing groups, perhaps most notably the Wash Wader Ringing Group.

Waders on a Florida beach

Golden Plovers

In recent years, growing concern for the environment and its wildlife has led to a greater interest and study of wading birds, particularly as much of the wetland habitat they use has been lost to development, and many other areas are under threat. In Britain the various proposed barrages across major estuaries have brought conservationists into conflict with developers, and never before have waders been such a matter of national and, indeed, international concern.

ALAN RICHARDS
1989

BREEDING SPECIES
OR
REGULAR MIGRANTS

Oystercatcher
Haematopus ostralegus   43cm

Nest   Scrape in shingle or sand
Egg clutch 2–4
Egg colour Spotted, blotched and streaked dark brown
Laid   Usually late May
Incubation 21–23 days
Fledging   28–35 days

Identification With its striking black and white plumage, pink legs, orange-red bill and blood-red eye, the distinctive Sea-pie, as it is sometimes called, is easily recognized. In flight it is equally distinctive, showing a broad white wing-bar with a white rump and tail. A gregarious species outside the breeding season, it can be seen feeding scattered over mudflats, or flying in long lines over the sea as it moves from feeding area to roosting place where they gather, often in their thousands.

Voice A shrill 'klee-eep klee-eep'; also utters a sharp 'pic-pic-pic'. Its song is a development of the 'klee-eep' note ending in a long kleepering trill.

Habitat Mainly coastal, it can be found on sandy or rocky shores alike. Also occurs along rivers and around inland lochs. On migration it can also be found around the margins of inland reservoirs (where it sometimes breeds). Frequently resorts to arable fields and moorland.

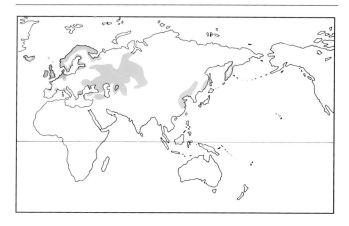

Food Molluscs form a major part of its diet, particularly cockles and mussels, which it prises open with its chisel-like bill. Also knocks limpets off rocks.

Range Breeds around the coasts of Europe, Asia and Africa, and can be found along Britain's coastline where suitable habitat allows, though sparse along north-east and southern coasts of England. Also nests around Irish coastline, except south.

Movements Most birds return to their breeding grounds in February and early March but continue to flock together before nesting begins in earnest. After nesting, birds move to estuaries and mudflats. Most British breeding birds, however, leave the country during winter.

RECORD OF SIGHTINGS	
Date _____	Date _____
Place _____	Place _____
Male(s) _____ Female(s) _____	Male(s) _____ Female(s) _____
Immature _____ Eclipse _____	Immature _____ Eclipse _____
Behaviour Notes	

Black-winged Stilt
Himantopus himantopus 35–40cm

Nest Can be shallow scrape on dry land or a substantial structure in shallow water
Egg clutch 4
Egg colour Stone-coloured, evenly spotted and blotched with dark brown
Laid May
Incubation 23 days
Fledging 28 days

Identification Readily indentified by its extremely long pink legs, needle-like black bill and simple black and white colour. A slender bird, most of its length is accounted for by legs and bill. The body is approximately the same size as most *Tringa* waders but has a somewhat diminutive head in addition to a long slim neck. The male is usually completely white-headed, while the female can have some black on it.
Voice Noisy excitable birds, they have a high pitched 'kik-kik-kik' alarm call. Also has a single 'kek' note uttered as a contact call.

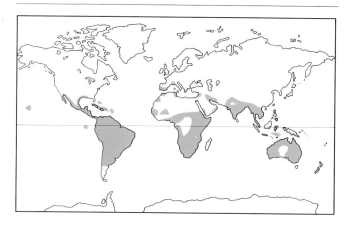

Habitat Fresh and salt-water marshes, lagoons, sewage farms, lakes.

Food Strides through shallow water seeking out all larval forms of insects, plus molluscs, worms and small fish.

Range Generally found in warmer climes. Main European breeding areas include Spain and southern France. Has nested irregularly in other European countries. In Britain bred successfully in 1987 after a gap of 42 years. Recently, the number of occurrences in spring and summer in Britain have increased, which may lead to further nesting records.

Movements Migratory in the northern part of its range, leaving Eurasia and northern America in the autumn for tropical quarters; returns to nesting areas, often migrating in pairs or social groups.

RECORD OF SIGHTINGS	
Date _____	Date _____
Place _____	Place _____
Male(s) _____ Female(s) _____	Male(s) _____ Female(s) _____
Immature _____ Eclipse _____	Immature _____ Eclipse _____
Behaviour Notes	

Avocet

Recurvirostra avosetta   42–45cm

Nest   A scrape lined with varying amounts of material
Egg clutch 3 or 4
Egg colour Pale buff, spotted irregularly with black and
               underlying ashy marks
Laid   Early May
Incubation 22–24 days
Fledging   35–42 days

Identification The contrasting black and white plumage, long
lead-blue legs and slender up-curved bill (which gives rise to the
local Norfolk name 'Awl-bird') are unmistakable. These features
combine to form one of Britain's most attractive wading birds,
making a great favourite with all who know it. When feeding, the
side-to-side sweeping action of the bird's bill is particularly
distinctive as it sieves the water-ooze for food. Probably even more
attractive when seen flying. It looks mainly white if viewed from
below, while the black and white wing-tips look less pointed than
those of most other wading birds.

Voice A noisy bird; on its breeding grounds has a penetrating
'kleet' or 'kluit' note.

Habitat Favours shallow brackish or saline estuaries, lakes,

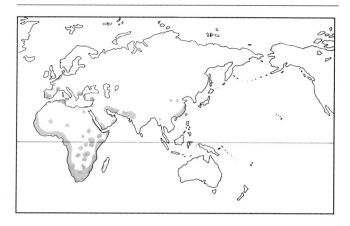

marshes and pools with water around 2–5cm in depth.

Food Small molluscs, crustaceans and worms, mainly located by touch as it wades, at times up to its belly; will also up-end like a duck. At other times will peck food from dry ground, or take insects from plants.

Range Breeds in western Europe from the British Isles and the Netherlands south to Spain and eastward spasmodically through to Asia. Also breeds in Africa.

Movements Mainly migratory, its British eastern breeding localities are deserted in winter. By October birds are to be found on estuaries along the English Channel and the southern North Sea coasts, with concentrations in Devon, Cornwall and Suffolk.

RECORD OF SIGHTINGS	
Date _____	Date _____
Place _____	Place _____
Male(s) _____ Female(s) _____	Male(s) _____ Female(s) _____
Immature ____ Eclipse _____	Immature ____ Eclipse _____
Behaviour Notes	

Stone-curlew

Burhinus oedicnemus   40−44cm

Nest   A shallow scrape in sand or soil
Egg clutch 2
Egg colour Pale buffish, heavily streaked and blotched dark brown
Laid   April−May
Incubation By both birds around 26 days
Fledging   5−6 weeks

Identification The upper body is light brown with darker and paler streaking, creating a cryptic pattern. An obvious feature in its plumage is a broad, light-grey patch on its wings. Its rear end is long and protruding, formed by a broad, long tail and folded wings. Most striking is the large piercing yellow eye. The bill is also yellow, short and sharply-tipped black. The legs are yellow and bulbous at the knee, hence the popular name 'Thick-knee'. In flight it shows a conspicuous double white wing bar. The sexes are similar.
Voice A shrill 'coor-lee'. A crepuscular species, it calls particularly towards dusk.
Habitat Dry semi-desert, heaths, dry cultivated land, downlands and the Brecklands of East Anglia.
Food It has a wide diet that includes beetles, woodlice,

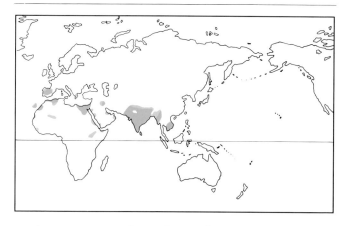

grasshoppers, worms and many insects all caught by a pecking motion. Will also stalk and catch mice, voles, lizards, frogs and sometimes the young of its neighbours.

Range Rather fragmented and worldwide, stretching from Europe to Asia. In Britain, mainly confined to a few counties in the south and east, with Suffolk and Norfolk particular strongholds. Has declined in recent years with now only about 200 pairs present throughout the summer. Mainly a summer visitor, a few may overwinter in southern England.

Movements Static over most of its range, except those breeding in Britain, France and Spain, most of which move to north Africa for the winter.

RECORD OF SIGHTINGS	
Date _____	Date _____
Place _____	Place _____
Male(s) _____ Female(s) _____	Male(s) _____ Female(s) _____
Immature _____ Eclipse _____	Immature _____ Eclipse _____
Behaviour Notes	

Little Ringed Plover
Charadrius dubius 14–17cm

Nest Scrape made by the male on dry ground
Egg clutch 4
Egg colour Buff to grey-green speckled with small brown-purplish spots
Laid April–May
Incubation 23 days
Fledging 23 days

Identification This bird always looks small-headed and has a generally nimbler manner and slimmer appearance compared to the larger-headed and rounder-bodied Ringed Plover. In both birds the upperparts are mid-brown and the underparts white, but this bird's black breast band is less extensive and the black facial mask is less intense. On close range the yellow orbital eye-ring immediately identifies the species. Additionally the flesh-coloured legs help put a name to it. When seen in flight, the lack of any wing bar is another distinguishing feature that separates it from the Ringed Plover.

Voice A shrill piping 'pew-pew'. On breeding grounds a trilling song like the Ringed Plover, accompanied by a similar butterfly-display flight.

Habitat Gravel pits, industrial spoil tips, waste ground, reservoir margins, stony or shingly stretches of rivers.

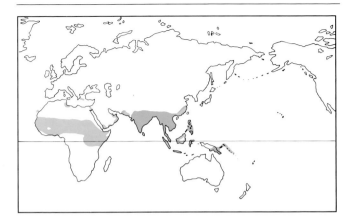

Food Various invertebrates, including worms, mosquito larvae, insect pupae, snails, beetles and, at times, the seeds of aquatic plants.

Range Breeds in Britain and Continental Europe, embracing central Scandinavia to the Mediterranean, and North Africa, then eastward through Asia to Japan, Borneo, and Papua New Guinea. Unknown in Britain before 1938, most are to be found in south-east England through to the east, west and north-east Midlands, Cheshire, Lancashire and parts of Yorkshire.

Movements A summer visitor, often arrives back in early March, departing for winter quarters in East and West Africa by September.

RECORD OF SIGHTINGS	
Date _____	Date _____
Place _____	Place _____
Male(s) _____ Female(s) _____	Male(s) _____ Female(s) _____
Immature _____ Eclipse _____	Immature _____ Eclipse _____
Behaviour Notes	

Ringed Plover

Charadrius hiaticula   18–20cm

Nest   A scrape in sand or shingle
Egg clutch 3 or 4 (sometimes two broods raised)
Egg colour Buff with blackish-brown speckles or blotches, usually
                concentrated at one end
Laid   April–May
Incubation 24–25 days
Fledging   24 days

Identification A small, rotund, lively shorebird, it has a prominent
black collar, broad at the front and narrow behind (which is
incomplete in the juvenile), a brown back and crown with a black
face and forehead. The legs are orange-yellow (flesh-coloured in
juveniles), and the bill is orange with a black tip. Normal flight is
rapid and generally low down, when a conspicuous white wing bar
is evident, a feature lacking on the similar Little Ringed Plover.
Voice A liquid 'pee-u'. Also has a piping 'kluup' call. The song is a
trilling 'tooli-tooli-tooli', to be heard regularly from March to July.
Habitat In the breeding season, sandy and shingly seashore. Also
nests on fallow land, dried mud of drained marshes near the coast,
sandy headland well away from the sea, inland rivers, lakes and
occasionally inland reservoir margins and gravel pits. Winters on

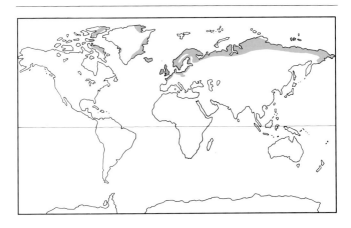

muddy and sandy estuaries. Frequently noted at inland waters on passage. In Britain nests in all suitable coastal areas, with its stronghold in the Outer Hebrides and high-density breeding in the Orkneys, Shetlands and Norfolk. Total breeding population probably 10,000 pairs.

Food Secures molluscs, worms or insects in typical plover fashion, taking one or two steps forward, or running to pick up whatever its keen sight has detected.

Range Breeds in Greenland, east to Baffin Island, Iceland and parts of western Europe north to Scandinavia.

Movements Many spend the winter on estuaries and mudflats, while others move to south-west Europe, especially Portugal.

RECORD OF SIGHTINGS	
Date _____	Date _____
Place _____	Place _____
Male(s) _____ Female(s) _____	Male(s) _____ Female(s) _____
Immature _____ Eclipse _____	Immature _____ Eclipse _____
Behaviour Notes	

Kentish Plover
Charadrius alexandrinus   15–17cm

Nest   Scrape in dry sandy ground
Egg clutch 3
Egg colour Pale buff with a sprinkling of black spots and streaks
Laid   Early May
Incubation 26 days
Fledging   28 days

Identification Smaller than a Ringed Plover, it has proportionally longer legs and a characteristically prominent head and shoulders body form. The upperparts are pale sandy in colour, with the breeding male displaying a small white forehead, black forecrown band and rufous-tinged hindcrown. Below the slim white brow, the black eyeband completes the head pattern. There is a characteristic black shoulder patch, which never forms a complete breast band. The underparts are wholly white. The female has the same patterning as the male, but the black areas are replaced by brown. The legs are dark grey, along with a short blackish bill. In flight shows a narrow white wing bar with white sides to the tail.
Voice A soft 'twit'.
Habitat Dune systems, saline coastal lagoons, inland steppe and

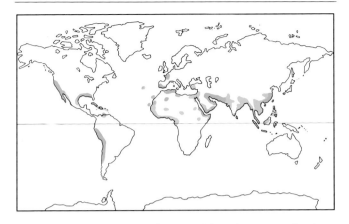

sand desert, also large sandy rivers and lakes where vegetation is at a minimum.

Food Small insects, molluscs, crustaceans and worms obtained in the usual plover manner: running, stopping, pecking in a fairly random fashion.

Range Virtually a continuous band through the warmer zones of the northern hemisphere.

Movements The continental interior populations are mainly migratory, whereas coastal breeding birds are more likely to be sedentary. Up to 40 pairs once bred in southern Britain from which the common name was derived. Now only a casual visitor and becoming rarer.

RECORD OF SIGHTINGS	
Date _____	Date _____
Place _____	Place _____
Male(s) _____ Female(s) _____	Male(s) _____ Female(s) _____
Immature _____ Eclipse _____	Immature _____ Eclipse _____
Behaviour Notes	

Dotterel
Charadrius morinellus   20–22cm

Nest   A shallow scrape
Egg clutch 2–4
Egg colour Greenish-buff blotched heavily reddish or
                blackish-brown
Laid   May or June
Incubation 26 days
Fledging   28 days

Identification Smaller than an adult Golden Plover, the Dotterel
is quite distinctive. The crown is dark and a conspicuous broad
white supercilium meets at the nape. The white cheeks and throat
are bordered by a medium-grey hind neck and upper chest. A slim
but prominent white breast band forms the upper demarcation line
to a rufous lower breast and black belly. The upperparts are mainly
dark with narrow buff and golden fringes to the feathers. The bill is
short and dark. The legs are dull yellowish. In flight shows no
marked features. The sexes are similar, though it is the female
which is the more brightly coloured of the pair. In winter adults
lose the rich coloration of the underparts. The juveniles look like
even paler version of the adults.
Voice A short trilling note on taking flight. Has a trilling song on
nesting grounds.
Habitat The breeding territory is sparsely vegetated upland,
especially raised tundra plateaux and 'whaleback' mountain ridges.

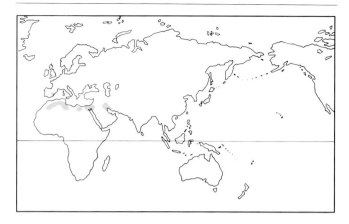

On migration regularly occurs at upland 'stopover' sites, large agricultural fields and coastal dunes.

Food Insects, worms, some molluscs and plant material as available. Feeding action typical of most plovers.

Range Widely distributed across Eurasia, with the mountains of Scandinavia and northern Siberia holding the majority of breeding birds. Smaller populations to be found in the Alps, Scotland and central Asia. In winter confined to the drier semi-desert zones of North Africa and the Middle East. An estimated 80 pairs nest in Britain.

Movements Leaves winter quarters in April when small groups or 'trips' migrate northwards. After nesting, birds fly south in July and August.

RECORD OF SIGHTINGS	
Date _____	Date _____
Place _____	Place _____
Male(s) _____ Female(s) _____	Male(s) _____ Female(s) _____
Immature _____ Eclipse _____	Immature _____ Eclipse _____
Behaviour Notes	

Golden Plover
Pluvialis apricaria   26–29cm

Nest	Scrape in low vegetation lined with heather stems and twigs
Egg clutch	4
Egg colour	Creamy-buff, occasionally pale green with blotches and spots of dark brown
Laid	May
Incubation	28 days
Fledging	25–33 days

Identification Smaller than a Lapwing, this bird has an oval body shape, shortish, dull-grey legs and a small dark bill. Predominantly a brown bird for most of the year, in spring adults become black on face and down the centre of the chest to the lower breast and belly. This is bordered by white, giving the underparts a smart pied appearance. The upperparts are spangled gold, which gives the bird its name. In flight the underwing and axillaries show a bright silvery white, a feature which distinguishes this bird from American and Pacific Golden Plovers.

Voice A plaintive 'tlu-i'. A liquid continuous trilling song on nesting grounds.

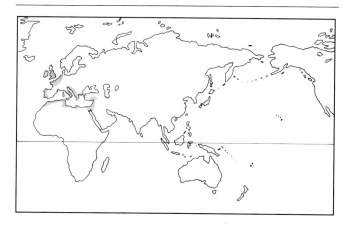

Habitat Open moorland, particularly with short heather in breeding season. In winter found on low elevation short grassland, agricultural fields and flat ground adjacent to estuaries.
Food Earthworms and beetles taken in typical plover fashion. Also seeds and berries on nesting ground.
Range Greenland and Iceland east across northern Europe to central Siberia. In winter Britain, France and Low Countries hold 80 per cent of the total world population. Other scattered winter sites include shores of Mediterranean south to Nile delta.
Movements Some British birds migrate to France and Iberia, but many move only 100 kilometres or so from breeding areas to wintering grounds.

RECORD OF SIGHTINGS	
Date _____	Date _____
Place _____	Place _____
Male(s) _____ Female(s) _____	Male(s) _____ Female(s) _____
Immature _____ Eclipse _____	Immature _____ Eclipse _____
Behaviour Notes	

Grey Plover
Pluvialis squatarola   27–31cm

Nest	Scrape on mossy lichen-covered ground
Egg clutch	4
Egg colour	Buffish-grey with darker spotting
Laid	End of May to late June in its more northerly limit
Incubation	23 days
Fledging	35–45 days

Identification In summer one of the most strikingly beautiful of shorebirds, its intense black underparts reach down to the belly. This black area is separated from the silvery-spangled grey and black upperparts by a broad band of pure white. The bill and legs are black. Closely resembling the Golden Plover in its winter colours, it is a somewhat larger and stouter-looking bird, with greyish-white underparts and silver-grey spangling instead of gold on the upperparts. In flight shows a bold white wing bar, white rump and distinctive black armpits (axillaries), which identify it immediately.

Voice A mournful, far-carrying 'tlee-oo-ee'.

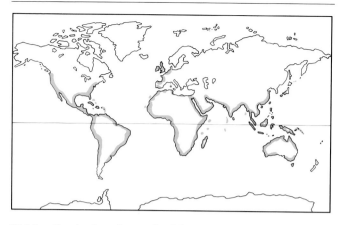

Habitat Lowland tundra north of the tree limit in breeding season, mudflats and estuaries in winter.

Food Worms, leather-jackets and a variety of inter-tidal invertebrates.

Range Nests almost continuously throughout the entire Arctic region of mainland Russia, Siberia and North America. Winters in Britain, where total population of around 20,000 birds represents about a third of the European population. Also occurs in France, Iberia and West Africa.

Movements Birds leave for breeding grounds in April and May, starting to return in July and August, with most arriving in September.

RECORD OF SIGHTINGS	
Date _____	Date _____
Place _____	Place _____
Male(s) _____ Female(s) _____	Male(s) _____ Female(s) _____
Immature _____ Eclipse _____	Immature _____ Eclipse _____
Behaviour Notes	

Lapwing
Vanellus vanellus 28–31cm

Nest   A simple scrape in earth, dry ground, or short
                  vegetation
Egg clutch   3 or 4, occasionally 5
Egg colour   Stone to brown, and covered with spots and blotches
                  of black
Laid   As early as March, but usually April/May
Incubation   28 days
Fledging   35–40 days

Identification At a distance looks very black and white, while
close observation will reveal the dark upperparts are metallic green
and the under-tail coverts a rufous buff (particularly obvious when
the bird comes in to land); the legs are reddish. At rest, the long
crest is very noticeable, and this is even more apparent in the male.
In flight the slow beats of the broad, rounded wings give a
distinctive flickering black and white appearance as the birds lazily
trail across the sky in straggling lines. Young birds have short crests
and pale edgings to the feathers, giving the upperparts a scaly look.
Voice A shrill, often wheezy-sounding 'pee-wit'. When displaying,
it has a longer drawn-out 'pee-weet-a-weet-weet' call, most

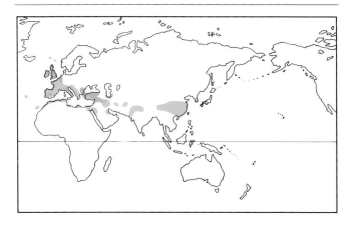

frequently uttered during its tumbling erratic nuptial flights in
March, April and May.

Habitat Found on arable land, newly ploughed fields, moorland,
rough ground, reservoir margins, and sand and gravel workings.
Less often found on mudflats or in other tidal situations.

Food Insects, worms, molluscs, crustacea and vegetable matter.

Range Breeds in Britain, Scandinavia and eastward across Europe
to Asia.

Movements Not usually known for its long migrations, many do,
however, move in the winter to escape bad weather. Generally hard
weather flights tend to be in a westerly direction, when many reach
Ireland. On rare occasions, crosses the Atlantic to North America.

RECORD OF SIGHTINGS	
Date _____	Date _____
Place _____	Place _____
Male(s) _____ Female(s) _____	Male(s) _____ Female(s) _____
Immature _____ Eclipse _____	Immature _____ Eclipse _____
Behaviour Notes	

Knot

Calidris canutus   23–25cm

Nest A scrape on dry rocky ground
Egg clutch 3 or 4
Egg colour Glossy, pale olive green with small brown markings
Laid June
Incubation 21 days
Fledging 20 days

Identification A stout, round, medium-sized bird with short, greenish-grey legs and black bill. It is well known for its large, communal gatherings and impressive aerial flights in its winter quarters. A plain, medium-grey above with an indistinct pale supercilium, the underparts are dull white, suffused with pale grey on the breast. In flight it shows an indistinct pale grey rump and a pencil-thin wing bar along its length. The change to summer plumage is most dramatic, as adults acquire rich orange-chestnut underparts from face to belly, while the upperparts become a mixture of black, white, chestnut and gold.
Voice 'Puk' or 'knut', hence the bird's name.
Habitat High Arctic tundra is the summer home, while large green mudflats which are backed by salt marshes and fields are the winter home.

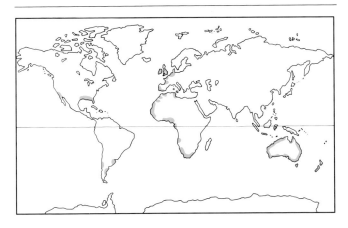

Food Mainly invertebrates, chiefly molluscs, crustaceans, worms and insects, plus larval insects and some plant material when on its breeding grounds.

Range Has a fragmented distribution throughout the Holarctic and the Canadian Islands, with Greenland and Siberia its main nesting strongholds.

Movements Leaves breeding grounds late July to early August, dispersing in four general directions. Heading south to South America, western Europe and West Africa, some find their way to Australia and New Zealand. Noted on spring and autumn passage, occasionally at inland waters. In Britain winter population of 200,000–300,000 birds is concentrated on all major estuaries.

RECORD OF SIGHTINGS	
Date _____	Date _____
Place _____	Place _____
Male(s) _____ Female(s) _____	Male(s) _____ Female(s) _____
Immature _____ Eclipse _____	Immature _____ Eclipse _____
Behaviour Notes	

Sanderling
Calidris alba 20–21cm

Nest   Scrape lined with small leaves or other vegetation
Egg clutch 4
Egg colour Greenish-olive, sometimes brownish, with sparse
               darker spotting
Laid   June
Incubation 28 days
Fledging   17 days

Identification About the same size as a Dunlin, the Sanderling is
rather more thickset with black legs and a short, straight, black bill.
One of the palest-looking waders during winter, with brilliant white
underparts, a bright silver back and a prominent black patch on the
inner wing at the shoulder. The dark eye shows up well on the
bird's almost white head. Summer plumage comprises a bright
chestnut colouring on the head, upper breast and upperparts. The
lower breast and belly remain bright white, while on the mantle
and scapulars, grey and white flecking is mixed in with the
chestnut colouring. Flight is fast and sometimes erratic, showing a
broad white bar along the wing.
Voice A distinctive 'twick'.
Habitat Flat tundra with some vegetation, usually in the proximity
of water during breeding season. At other times prefers long, sandy
beaches.
Food Adult and larval dipteran flies, small beetles, sandhoppers,
spiders and burrowing amphipods. On breeding ground also eats
plant buds, seeds, algae and mosses.

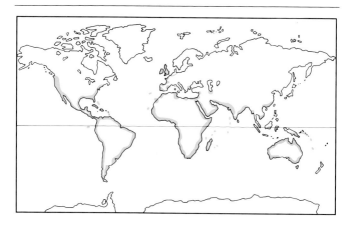

Range Breeds in three major areas: Arctic Canada, Greenland and Siberia. To be found on virtually any suitable beach throughout the world when not nesting.

Movements Birds leave their breeding grounds in late July to mid-August, appearing on both east and west coasts during the autumn passage period. In spring movement back to nesting territories begins March and April, continuing until May. When Sanderling pass through Britain in spring and autumn, small numbers appear at inland locations, especially in spring. Not as numerous as some waders around British coasts, the winter population is probably around 8000 individuals, representing about 80 per cent of the European population.

RECORD OF SIGHTINGS	
Date _____	Date _____
Place _____	Place _____
Male(s) _____ Female(s) _____	Male(s) _____ Female(s) _____
Immature _____ Eclipse _____	Immature _____ Eclipse _____
Behaviour Notes	

Little Stint
Calidris minuta   12–14cm

Nest   A shallow cup lined with leaves and grass
Egg clutch 4
Egg colour Pale green, boldly blotched with brown
Laid   Late June, early July
Incubation 21 days
Fledging   17–18 days

Identification Noticeably smaller than the commoner Dunlin, the
Little Stint has a shorter, finer black bill and black legs. Birds in
breeding plumage have rufous heads, necks and breasts with brown
streaks. The black back feathers have bright rufous edges, which
add to their smart appearance. The underparts are white, except for
a buff wash and slight streaking on the upper breast. In winter
adults are basically brownish-grey above and white underneath.
Juveniles have a dark rufous crown, which is accentuated by lateral
white stripes and bold, white supercilia. Their napes are grey and
their dark upper feathers are fringed rufous and white with very
distinctive white edges to the mantle, which forms a marked V on
their backs. The underparts are again white, except for a buff
breast, which is streaked at the sides. In flight there is a clear white
wing bar and white sides on the rump and tail.

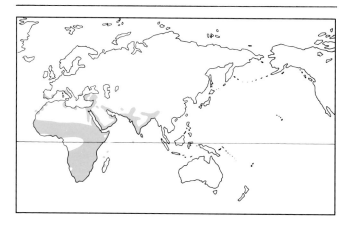

Voice Usual call is a short, low pitched 'tit' or 'chit'.
Habitat Breeds in the Arctic tundra. At other times, mainly coastal, though some do occur inland.
Food Invertebrates, such as insects, beetles, worms and small molluscs and crustaceans.
Range Nests in Scandinavia and northern Russia. Most winter in Africa, around the Mediterranean, or in India.
Movements Move northwards to their breeding grounds between April and early June; a few pass through Britain at this time. After nesting, adults return southwards, followed in late August by juveniles. Passage often continues into October. A few overwinter.

RECORD OF SIGHTINGS	
Date _____	Date _____
Place _____	Place _____
Male(s) _____ Female(s) _____	Male(s) _____ Female(s) _____
Immature _____ Eclipse _____	Immature _____ Eclipse _____
Behaviour Notes	

Temminck's Stint
Calidris temminckii 13−15cm

Nest Shallow depression scantily lined with grass or leaves
Egg clutch 4
Egg colour Greenish, with dark markings
Laid June
Incubation 21 days
Fledging 14−21 days

Identification A tiny mouse-like wader, distinguished from other small sandpipers and stints by its plain dull appearance. In breeding plumage the mantle and scapular feathers have black centres and buff edges which give it a darker, drabber appearance than the Little Stint. The head and breast are mottled and streaked brown on a grey background, the chin and belly are white, and there is an indistinct pale supercilium. Non-breeding birds are more uniform. In flight shows a short, narrow, white wing bar, also white sides to rump and distinctive white outer tail feathers; most obvious on take-off and when landing.
Voice A quick dry 'tirrirrirri' rattle, usually uttered when flushed, at which time frequently 'towers' like Common Snipe.
Habitat Tundra with short turfy areas or sandy, gravelly shorelines of freshwater pools and islets, also sheltered valleys with plenty of

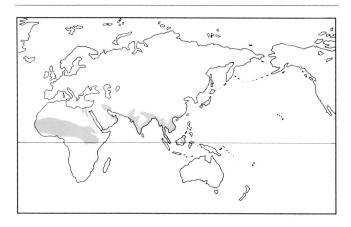

mossy bogs, damp grassland and dwarf willow scrub for nesting. At other times, sheltered muddy backwaters and saltmarshes, inland waters, irrigated areas, but rarely on coast.

Food Insects and their larvae, especially beetles and flies.

Range From Norway to north-eastern Siberia. Some nest in southern Scandinavia, and three or four pairs nest annually in Scotland. Main wintering areas are the northern tropics, but a few remain in Europe as far north as Britain.

Movements Birds return northwards and pass through Europe between mid-April and mid-May. Southward passage is quite leisurely, beginning when adults leave in July and continuing until the juveniles reach their wintering grounds in October.

RECORD OF SIGHTINGS	
Date _____	Date _____
Place _____	Place _____
Male(s) _____ Female(s) _____	Male(s) _____ Female(s) _____
Immature ____ Eclipse _____	Immature ____ Eclipse _____
Behaviour Notes	

Pectoral Sandpiper

Calidris melanotos 19–23cm

Nest	On ground and well hidden, made of grass, leaves and lichen
Egg clutch	4
Egg colour	Greenish to buff, heavily blotched with brown
Laid	June
Incubation	21–23 days
Fledging	21 days

Identification A medium-sized sandpiper, the males are significantly larger than the females. At all times, marked by a neat, well-streaked breast or pectoral band which is characteristically cut off from the white underparts. The bill is medium length and slightly down-curved, the basal third being olive-coloured. The legs are olive to yellow in colour. In breeding plumage adults show a mixture of black, grey and buff upperparts with black scapulars neatly fringed with buff. There is a white V at the side of the mantle. In winter plumage the feather centres are duller, with dingier, ill-defined fringes. Juveniles are similar to summer adults but have rather darker feather centres and better defined white, russet and buff fringes, giving a neater, crisp effect. There are usually two prominent white Vs on the side of the mantle and scapulars. In flight there is a narrow, white wing bar, while the

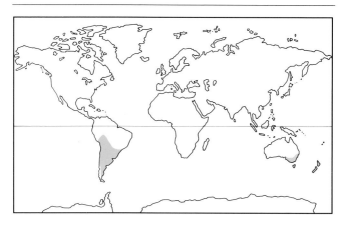

black centre to the rump and tail shows a prominent white area at the sides.

Voice On breeding ground a hooting 'oo-af' call; at other times, a harsh, reedy 'churk' or 'prrp'.

Habitat Wet, flat tundra, both on coast and in foothills.

Food Insects, worms, flies, insect larvae; sometimes crickets, grasshoppers and fiddler-crabs; occasionally some vegetable matter.

Range Breeds in eastern Siberia to Hudson Bay. Almost the entire population winters in South America. Small numbers winter regularly in Australia and New Zealand. Also occurs as a vagrant in Hawaii, South Africa and western Europe. This species is the most frequent transatlantic vagrant in western Europe and is regularly noted each autumn in Britain.

RECORD OF SIGHTINGS	
Date _____	Date _____
Place _____	Place _____
Male(s) _____ Female(s) _____	Male(s) _____ Female(s) _____
Immature ____ Eclipse _____	Immature ____ Eclipse _____
Behaviour Notes	

Curlew Sandpiper
Calidris ferruginea   18–23cm

Nest　　　A shallow depression in a grass tussock
Egg clutch 4
Egg colour Olive buff or greenish-grey, with bold brown blotches
　　　　　　and spots
Laid　　　June
Incubation Not known
Fledging　 Not known

Identification Similar in size to a Dunlin but more delicately built
and elegant in behaviour. Its long, decurved black bill, slender neck
and long black legs produce a characteristic outline. Breeding adults
have rich chestnut heads, necks and underparts, apart from their
undertail coverts, which are white. The upperparts are a mixture of
black feathers with chestnut fringes and white tips on the scapulars,
while the wing coverts are grey-brown with whitish fringes.
Females have paler underparts, with some white feathers and dark
brown barring on the belly. In non-breeding plumage it is grey-
brown above and white below. There is a long, white supercilium.
Juveniles are similar to non-breeding birds but have browner
upperparts, with a scaly appearance and a buff wash to the neck
and breast. The flight is swift, showing their white wing bars and
distinctive white rump.
Voice A characteristic rippling 'chirrup'.
Habitat Favoured breeding area is Arctic tundra with an
abundance of rich boggy pools and hollows fed by melting snow. In
winter it favours both muddy and sandy shores, tidal creeks and the
muddy margins of freshwater pools.

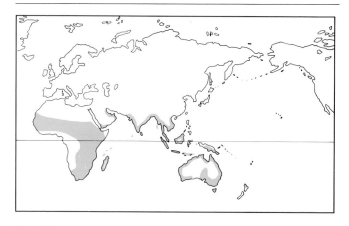

Food Crustaceans, molluscs, insects and some vegetable matter.
Range Breeds in a small area from the Yenisei river eastwards to
the Kolyma delta, but also occasionally in northern Alaska. Main
wintering area extends from West Africa through to India, south-
east Asia and Australasia.
Movements In spring birds follow a direct route from winter
quarters in Africa across Italy and south-eastern Europe, hence few
are seen in Britain in their spectacular breeding plumage. Return
passage can begin as early as late June when the first males leave.
Females follow in July. Juveniles are the last to leave in August.
Regular autumn visitor to Britain with variable numbers from year
to year.

RECORD OF SIGHTINGS	
Date _____	Date _____
Place _____	Place _____
Male(s) _____ Female(s) _____	Male(s) _____ Female(s) _____
Immature ____ Eclipse _____	Immature ____ Eclipse _____
Behaviour Notes	

Purple Sandpiper
Calidris maritima   20–22cm

Nest   Small cup shaped in tundra vegetation
Egg clutch 4
Egg colour Greenish, blotched and spotted dark brown with some blackish lines
Laid   June
Incubation 21 days
Fledging   Probably 3–4 weeks

Identification At all times a dark-plumaged, portly bird with quite a long, yellow-based, drooping bill and short yellow legs. In winter is dark slate-grey on the head, neck, back and wings, and on much of the upper breast. Slim paler fringes are evident on the coverts and tertials, while adults show a small white chin. The belly and undertail coverts are whitish, often flecked with grey at the sides. At times the upperparts have a purple hue, hence the name. In summer the basic plumage remains dark but takes on a browner tone, with the crown and scapulars becoming more scaly-looking, being edged with gold, chestnut and white. There is a pale, indistinct supercilium. Juvenile plumage is not unlike adult's summer dress. In flight the dark tail is bordered by bright white, lateral upper tail coverts; there is a slim white wing bar.

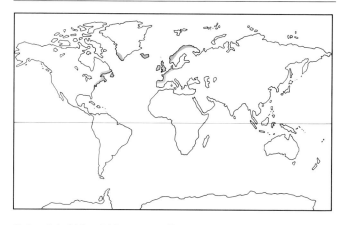

Voice A 'whit' or 'tit' contact call.

Habitat Breeds on the Arctic tundra. Spends the whole winter on low rocky coasts; sometimes to be found on jetties, piers and breakwaters, and very occasionally sandy or muddy shores.

Food Small molluscs, crustaceans, algae, worms and insects.

Range Breeds on the Canadian islands near Siberia, as well as Iceland and upland Scandinavia. Most Canadian birds winter on the north-east coast of North America, though some are found around the Great Lakes.

Movements Few Palearctic birds move any distance, and usually no further south than Portugal. Iceland and Scandinavia are the main wintering areas.

RECORD OF SIGHTINGS	
Date _____	Date _____
Place _____	Place _____
Male(s) _____ Female(s) _____	Male(s) _____ Female(s) _____
Immature _____ Eclipse _____	Immature _____ Eclipse _____
Behaviour Notes	

Dunlin
Calidris alpina   16–22cm

Nest   Small depression well hidden in vegetation
Egg clutch 4
Egg colour Pale greenish to olive-buff with grey spots
Laid   April, May or June, depending on latitude
Incubation 22 days
Fledging   20 days

Identification A small, dumpy, highly active bird generally
considered the 'yardstick' against which many other small waders
can be compared. During the winter a dull, grey-brown bird, the
upperparts rather plain, while the breast is lightly streaked grey
with the remainder of the underparts white. In breeding plumage
its large black belly patch contrasts with white vent and flank and
darker-streaked breast, while the black-centred mantle and scapular
feathers show varying bright chestnut, grey and white borders. The
legs are medium length and black. The bill is long, black and drooped
at the tip. In flight shows a conspicuous narrow white wing bar,
white sides to the rump and upper tail, and a white underwing.
There are six races of the Dunlin. The races *schinzii* and *arctica* are
the smallest. These occur in Britain, together with *alpina*.
Voice A shrill 'treep' or 'kree' call.
Habitat Can be found in a variety of nesting situations, from
saltings and machair to peat moorland upwards of 1200 metres. In
winter prefers extensive areas of tidal mudflats or anywhere with
mud-fringed water.
Food Inter-tidal invertebrates, including rag worms, bivalves and
small molluscs, and planktonic crustacea during the winter. On

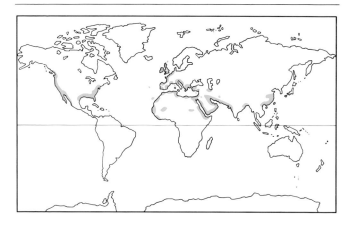

breeding grounds eats adult and larval insects, beetles, spiders, mites, earthworms and sometimes seeds.

Range Circumpolar in its breeding distribution. The nominate race *alpina* breeds in northern Scandinavia and north-west USSR, wintering in western Europe and the Mediterranean east to India. The race *schinzii* breeds in south-east Greenland, Iceland, Britain and southern Scandinavia, while *arctica* breeds in north-east Greenland and winters mainly in West Africa.

Movements Returns to breeding grounds in April or May, and leaves after nesting from July onwards. Migration can extend into November. About 500,000 birds winter along the shores of Britain. These are birds that have bred further north and they represent about half the western European population.

RECORD OF SIGHTINGS	
Date _____	Date _____
Place _____	Place _____
Male(s) _____ Female(s) _____	Male(s) _____ Female(s) _____
Immature _____ Eclipse _____	Immature _____ Eclipse _____
Behaviour Notes	

Ruff

Philomachus pugnax 26–32cm (male)
20–25cm (female)

Nest A well-concealed shallow scrape lined with grass
Egg clutch 4
Egg colour Greenish-olive, blotched and streaked with brown
Laid May
Incubation 20–23 days
Fledging 25–28 days

Identification A medium to large bird with a small head, long neck, medium-length, slightly decurved bill and long legs. The males are much larger than females. During the breeding season the male is particularly distinctive, with an Elizabethan-style ruff and ear tufts whose colours vary from individual to individual, from white through buff and rusty to black, either barred or plain. The bill and legs are yellow to red. Females in breeding plumage are also variable in appearance but have a dark brown head, breast and upperparts, with many dark feather centres and dark spotting on the breast and flanks. Juveniles have neatly scaled upperparts with blackish feather centres, especially in the scapulars, fringed buff to white. The bill is black and legs blackish. In flight all Ruffs show prominent white ovals at the sides of the rump and a white wing bar.
Voice Generally silent, but very occasionally utters a quiet 'tu-whit'.
Habitat In breeding seasons is found in low-lying tundra with lakes and marshes, or damp grasslands and meadow in the more

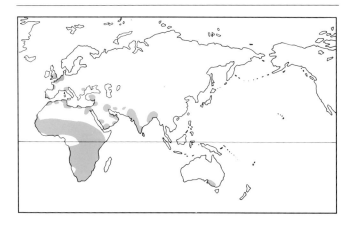

southern parts of its range. On passage and in winter favours grassland, freshwater margins, paddies and coastal lagoons. Rarely on coast.

Food Chiefly insects, also worms, small freshwater molluscs and small crustaceans; also vegetable matter at times.

Range Breeds across northern Europe and Asia from the British Isles to eastern Siberia. Virtually the entire Ruff population winters in Africa, mostly in a strip from Senegal and Gambia to Sudan.

Movements A common migrant throughout Europe, northward passage starts in February and lasts until May. Autumn movement begins with the usual protracted passage of males from early July, followed by females and juveniles lasting until October.

RECORD OF SIGHTINGS	
Date _____	Date _____
Place _____	Place _____
Male(s) _____ Female(s) _____	Male(s) _____ Female(s) _____
Immature _____ Eclipse _____	Immature _____ Eclipse _____
Behaviour Notes	

Jack Snipe

Limnocryptes minimus   17–19cm

Nest   A shallow cup lined with grass on tussock
Egg clutch 4
Egg colour Olive to dark brown, heavily blotched with chestnut
Laid   May
Incubation 24 days
Fledging   Probably 3 weeks

Identification Much smaller than Common Snipe, with a
relatively shorter bill, it is notoriously difficult to see on the
ground. Usually reluctant to fly, when flushed rises silently, not
zigzagging like the commoner bird, to land after a short distance.
Crown pattern differs from Common Snipe, lacking the pale central
stripe and having one on either side separated by black border from
a less prominent pale stripe over the eye. The general plumage has
more metallic green and purple gloss, and flanks show dark
mottling instead of distinct bar. The legs are greenish. Several birds

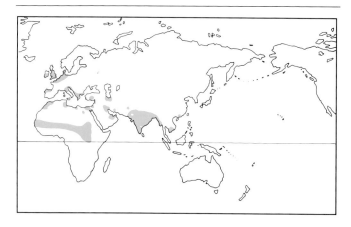

may be found in a favoured area but always rise separately when flushed.

Voice Rarely if ever calls when flushed.

Habitat Marshy wetlands, usually among conifers in breeding season. In winter, boggy marsh areas, but sometimes in quite dry locations.

Food Worms, small land and freshwater molluscs, also insects and their larvae, and some vegetable matter.

Range Breeds from northern Norway eastwards across Scandinavia through to Siberia in a thick belt stretching to the Arctic tree-line.

Movements Birds return to their breeding grounds between April and mid-May. By early September the breeding grounds are deserted and migrants have reached winter quarters by October.

RECORD OF SIGHTINGS	
Date _____	Date _____
Place _____	Place _____
Male(s) _____ Female(s) _____	Male(s) _____ Female(s) _____
Immature _____ Eclipse _____	Immature _____ Eclipse _____
Behaviour Notes	

Common Snipe
Gallinago gallinago   25–27cm

Nest   A well-hidden scrape lined with grasses
Egg clutch   4
Egg colour   Olive-grey blotched with dark brown and black
Laid   April–May
Incubation   18–19 days
Fledging   Around 15 days

Identification Usually seen as a silhouette when it explodes from cover, flying off in an erratic zigzag manner. If observed on the ground, the plumage is seen to be a mixture of rich browns, blacks and yellows. The upperparts are heavily mottled and barred, the colours producing the effect of longitudinal stripes. The crown is black with a central buff streak above and below the eye. The eye is set high up in the head, thus allowing the bird all-round vision as it probes for food with the full length of its long, straight bill. The

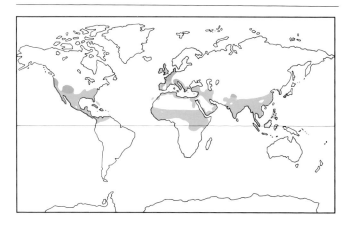

legs and feet are pale green, while the bill is brown. The sexes are similar.

Voice A harsh 'scaap' note uttered as it flies when startled.

Habitat From lowland marshy ground to more elevated boggy moorland. Sometimes in much drier locations.

Food Worms and a wide variety of invertebrates, plus insects and their larvae; at times seeds are eaten.

Range There are three races of Snipe. The nominate race *gallinago* is to be found throughout most of the Palearctic, while *faeroeensis* breeds in Iceland, the Faroes, Orkney and the Shetlands. The race *delicata* or Wilson's Snipe, breeds throughout North America.

Movements Little evidence of any extensive migrations, but considerable winter influx of birds from the Baltic.

RECORD OF SIGHTINGS	
Date _____	Date _____
Place _____	Place _____
Male(s) _____ Female(s) _____	Male(s) _____ Female(s) _____
Immature _____ Eclipse _____	Immature _____ Eclipse _____
Behaviour Notes	

Great Snipe
Gallinago media   27–29cm

Nest Shallow depression lined with some grass, well hidden
Egg clutch 4
Egg colour Fawn to buff, with dark brown blotches or spots at the broad end
Laid 22–24 days
Fledging 3–4 weeks

Identification Very similar in appearance to Common Snipe, both on ground and in the air, but a bulkier bird with a ball-shaped body, a larger head and a slightly shorter bill. The head stripes are less prominent, while on the wing coverts, white spots are conspicuous, forming parallel rows across the closed wing. The flanks and most of the belly are barred with dark chevrons, a clear difference from Common Snipe. Juveniles are duller-looking. The flight is characteristically short, low, unhurried and direct compared to the frantic, towering zigzagging of the commoner bird. Another distinguishing feature is that the shorter bill is carried nearer the horizontal. Other points to look for on the wing are the adult's mid-wing panel bordered by lines of striking white spots, and conspicuous white corners to the tail.
Voice If it calls at all, it utters a low weak 'urrgh'.
Habitat Generally prefers boggy ground near the tree-line for

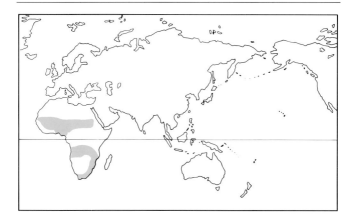

nesting, but also chooses many sorts of marshland, though usually with some trees nearby; may even nest in quite dry woodland. In the main favours drier sites than Common Snipe.

Food Earthworms, small snails and slugs, a variety of insects and some marsh plant seeds.

Range Breeds in Scandinavia and eastern Poland to the river Yenisey in Siberia. In winter most are to be found south to the Equator, especially in Zambia and Malawi. In Britain an occasional autumn visitor, with a few spring records; less frequent than in former years.

Movements The breeding areas are deserted from mid-August onwards, with birds passing through central and eastern Europe *en route* to Africa. Return to breeding grounds in May.

RECORD OF SIGHTINGS	
Date _____	Date _____
Place _____	Place _____
Male(s) _____ Female(s) _____	Male(s) _____ Female(s) _____
Immature ____ Eclipse _____	Immature ____ Eclipse _____
Behaviour Notes	

Woodcock
Scolopax rusticola   33–35cm

Nest	A shallow depression lined with leaves
Egg clutch	4
Egg colour	Glossy, greyish-white to warm brown, spotted or streaked with darker brown
Laid	March–April
Incubation	21 days
Fledging	35–42 days

Identification In outline resembles a heavily-built Snipe, with a similar long straight bill. However, is bulkier with broad, rounded wings and is normally found in quite a different habitat. Superficially the plumage shows the same mixtures of rufous browns, buffs and blacks as Snipe, but the Woodcock's head has transverse black bars and it lacks the other bird's distinctive buff stripes on its back. The Woodcock's large eye is also set very high up in the head, which gives it a most distinctive appearance. Largely active at dusk, it is most likely to be seen during the course of its roding display flights from March through to July. Each dawn and dusk the male traverses a variable circuit above the tree-tops, flying quite fast but with slow, owl-like wing action, calling as it goes.

Voice A low croaking sound, also a thin 'tsiwick' note uttered in both roding and non-roding flight.

Habitat Damp lowland woods and forests with good shrub layer or an under-storey of bracken.

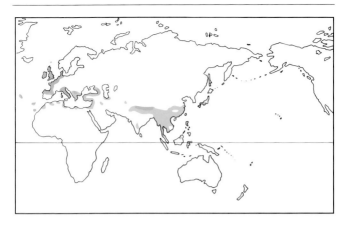

Food Largely earthworms, but also insects and their larvae; at times vegetable matter is eaten.

Range Breeding area extends right across the temperate forest zone of Eurasia. Winters in Britain, Ireland and France, where it overlaps with breeding area; also moves south to Iberia and North Africa, and from Asia Minor to Japan.

Movements Birds disperse from breeding grounds at the onset of hard weather, which takes place quite late from October and November, even through to December. The general movement is south and west across its range. This westerly migration has led to vagrancy across the Atlantic, with records from Newfoundland and Quebec, south to Alabama and inland in Ohio.

RECORD OF SIGHTINGS	
Date _____	Date _____
Place _____	Place _____
Male(s) _____ Female(s) _____	Male(s) _____ Female(s) _____
Immature ____ Eclipse _____	Immature ____ Eclipse _____
Behaviour Notes	

Black-tailed Godwit
Limosa limosa 36–44cm

Nest	A shallow scrape in short vegetation lined with grass or leaves
Egg clutch	3 or 4
Egg colour	Olive brown with dark markings
Laid	May
Incubation	21 days
Fledging	28 days or more

Identification A long-billed, long-legged, graceful shorebird, the male in summer has a chestnut-coloured head and breast, while the belly and flanks are white with distinct black bars. The female, though similarly coloured, is duller-looking. In winter both sexes are basically grey and white but the flight pattern is always distinctive, with its strong white wing bar, white tail with broad black terminal band, and trailing legs identifying it immediately. Juveniles have a warm pink or buff tinge to the upperparts and breast reminiscent of a pale adult in breeding dress. Frequently wades up to its belly to feed, at other times probes the soft sand or mud. Generally, only found in small groups, but flocks several hundred strong can occur in favoured localities.

Voice A clear 'wicka-wicka-wicka' uttered by birds in flight.

Habitat Nests among damp vegetation, but at other times occurs around muddy margins of fresh water, in flooded fields and in favoured estuaries or river valleys in winter.

Food Worms, molluscs and crustaceans.

Range There are three separate races. The European and western Asiatic race breeds in an area stretching from Britain across to central Russia, wintering mainly in Africa and India. The Icelandic race breeds in Iceland and winters in western Europe, especially Britain and Ireland. A third race breeds in eastern Asia and winters south to Australia. The western European population is centred on

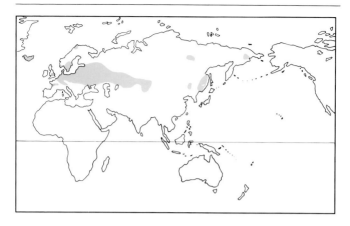

the Low Countries and West Germany. In Britain the species became extinct about 150 years ago, but began to recolonize the Ouse Washes in East Anglia in the 1950s. Since then, it has established a firm foothold there and has spread to new areas, though with no more than 80 pairs at a dozen widely-scattered sites, it remains scarce and local. The British migrant population has also increased.

Movements Northwards migration takes place between February and April, with European birds arriving from Africa a month or so before birds wintering in Britain leave for Iceland. Return passage begins in late June, when adults leave breeding grounds. Juveniles follow, and by August the breeding grounds are deserted.

RECORD OF SIGHTINGS

Date _____	Date _____
Place _____	Place _____
Male(s) _____ Female(s) _____	Male(s) _____ Female(s) _____
Immature _____ Eclipse _____	Immature _____ Eclipse _____

Behaviour Notes

Bar-tailed Godwit
Limosa lapponica 37–41cm

Nest A shallow depression lined with a few twigs and dead leaves

Egg clutch 3 or 4

Egg colour A light background with sparse grey markings and brown blotches

Laid June

Incubation 21 days

Fledging 28 days

Identification In winter plumage confusion with the Black-tailed Godwit is possible, but the slightly browner and more heavily streaked upperparts and dull white underparts, as well as the shorter, all-dark legs, long, slightly uptilted bill and more dumpy appearance are useful differences. In breeding dress the head, neck and underparts are a deep rufous-cinnamon or chestnut colour, with the darker central mantle and scapulars showing orangy-buff edgings, but the wing coverts stay a duller grey-brown. The female remains duller-looking, only developing a warm buff-wash down the throat and breast. In flight the rather uniform brown wings, barred tail and contrasting white rump and lower back are further aids to its identification.

Voice A sharp 'kak-kak' or 'kirrick'.

Habitat Low-lying swamp tundra for breeding. Mudflats and tidal estuaries in winter.

Food Annelid worms, crustaceans, molluscs, insects, caterpillars, also berries and seeds on nesting grounds.

Range Northern Scandinavia eastwards to the westernmost part of

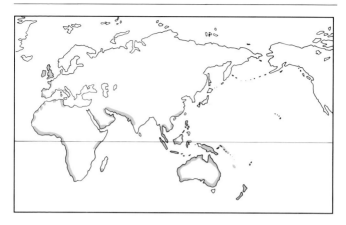

Alaska close to the Arctic Circle between latitudes 65° and 75°
north. Winters along the shores well to the south in Africa, with a
sporadic distribution to India, south-east Asia and Australia.
Concentrations of up to 600,000 birds are recorded in Mauritania,
north-west Africa, while 60 per cent of birds remaining in Europe
are found around British coasts.

Movements Adults depart from their breeding grounds in late
June and July, with birds of the year following soon afterwards.
Migration southwards to traditional autumn moulting grounds,
such as the Ribble and the Wash estuaries in Britain, and the
Waddenzee in the Netherlands, is fairly rapid. In spring birds pass
northward equally rapidly during late April and May.

RECORD OF SIGHTINGS	
Date _____	Date _____
Place _____	Place _____
Male(s) _____ Female(s) _____	Male(s) _____ Female(s) _____
Immature _____ Eclipse _____	Immature _____ Eclipse _____
Behaviour Notes	

Whimbrel

Numenius phaeopus 40–46cm

Nest	Scrape on short tussocky vegetation
Egg clutch	4
Egg colour	Olive-brown, spotted and blotched brown and lavender
Laid	May–June
Incubation	27–28 days
Fledging	35–42 days

Identification At first glance similar to the Curlew, but the boldly patterned head, shorter, more sharply decurved bill and smaller size all suggest it is a different species. The combination of pale buff central crown stripe and eyebrows, contrasting strongly with darker sides to crown and eye stripe, are particularly distinctive. The upperparts appear slightly darker brown than the Curlew, with variably marked paler fringes giving a more mottled appearance at a distance. The white upper tail, rump and back contrast with the rest of the upperparts and the tail, which is grey-brown with darker barring. The underparts are buffish-white, variably streaked with darker brown on the breast. Juveniles look similar to adults but the crown is darker, showing less contrast with lateral crown stripes and eyebrows.

Voice A rapid, tittering of even emphasis, often repeated seven times, hence common name 'Seven Whistler'. Song is a trill.

Habitat For nesting prefers open tundra or comparatively dry moorland with perhaps the occasional stunted tree. In winter a coastal species, haunting mudflats, beaches and estuaries.

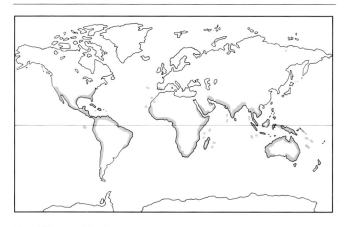

Food Has a wide diet includes molluscs, crustaceans and annelids or snails, beetles and earthworms as available. Seeds and berries are also eaten at times.

Range Virtually circumpolar as a breeding bird. Icelandic, north European and central Siberian nesting birds winter in the Afro-tropics and along the west coasts of the Indian Ocean.

Movements From late July, passage birds head south for winter quarters, generally along a broad front. Most frequently observed along the coast. Inland, most records are of birds passing overhead, often at night. Return passage in spring is mainly in April and May. The North American race *hudsonia*, identifiable by its brown rump, is a vagrant to Britain and has been recorded on four occasions up to 1986.

RECORD OF SIGHTINGS	
Date _____	Date _____
Place _____	Place _____
Male(s) _____ Female(s) _____	Male(s) _____ Female(s) _____
Immature _____ Eclipse _____	Immature _____ Eclipse _____
Behaviour Notes	

Curlew
Numenius arquata 51–60cm

Nest Scrape in grass or heather
Egg clutch 4
Egg colour Glossy greenish to dark brown, with speckles, blotches and streaks of brown
Laid May/June
Incubation 28 days
Fledging 6 weeks

Identification The largest of European shorebirds, 10–15cm of its length is taken up by the distinctive curved bill, the longest-billed birds being female. The head, neck and breast are light brown with dark streakings, while the underparts are whitish with streaks and transverse barring to the flanks. There is brown barring on the tail and the long legs are greenish-grey. In flight, which is slow and relatively gull-like compared to other waders, the whitish rump extending up the back is a distinctive feature, for there are no wing bars.

Voice A far-reaching 'cur-lee', which gives the bird its name. On the breeding grounds the call extends into a high-pitched bubbling trill.

Habitat In Britain is very much a bird of upland areas in the breeding season, but also favours lowland locations, damp meadows, and especially grassland in river valleys. Outside breeding season haunts mudflats, saltings and estuaries, as well as sandy and rocky shores. Frequently found inland on migration.

Food Ragworms, molluscs and small crabs; on breeding grounds worms, insects, seeds and berries.

Range During the breeding season found in temperate and sub-

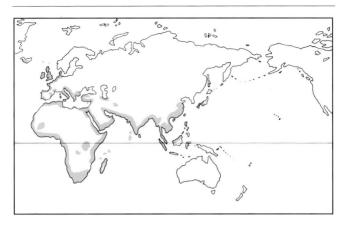

Arctic regions from Britain eastwards to Siberia, and from
Scandinavia and Russia in the north to France through to the
Balkans and beyond to the Khirghiz steppes. In winter occurs from
northern Europe to the Atlantic Isles in the west, south to South
Africa and Madagascar, and east to India and south-east Asia.
Movements In spring birds return to breeding ground as early as
February in lowland Britain. In higher latitudes it is probably May,
or even early June, before nesting is properly under way. By the
end of July most breeding areas are deserted and birds return to
their winter quarters. In Britain the winter population is
supplemented by migrants from central and eastern Europe, though
many pass through *en route* to France and Spain.

RECORD OF SIGHTINGS	
Date _____	Date _____
Place _____	Place _____
Male(s) _____ Female(s) _____	Male(s) _____ Female(s) _____
Immature _____ Eclipse _____	Immature _____ Eclipse _____
Behaviour Notes	

Spotted Redshank
Tringa erythropus 29–32cm

Nest   A shallow depression lined with leaves, stems and feathers
Egg clutch 4
Egg colour Greenish, streaked, blotched or finely marked all over with reddish-brown
Laid   June
Incubation 23 days
Fledging 4 or 5 weeks

Identification In winter plumage may be mistaken for Redshank, but has a larger, more slender neck and long, attenuated rear end, as opposed to the more dumpy, rounded commoner bird. The upperparts are much clearer in appearance, formed by a light grey base interspersed by uniformly white-edged feathers. A thick black stripe through the eye emphasizes a very white eyebrow. The underparts are whiter with finer streaking. The bill and legs are much longer, the latter usually being dark red. In flight there is a white rump with no white in the wings. In breeding dress it is unmistakable, with sooty-black plumage evenly sprinkled with small bright white spots over its back and wings, this 'peppered' look giving rise to the name.

Habitat Nests in open marshy areas but also favours dry areas among forest marshes. In winter mostly found on coastal and freshwater lagoons. On migration occurs at inland locations around the edges of reservoirs and pools.

Food Worms, crustaceans, insect larvae, also water beetles, newts

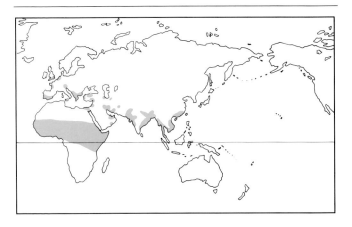

and small frogs; on breeding grounds frantically chases and snatches newly-hatched mosquitos.

Range Breeds from northern Sweden eastwards to eastern Siberia. Mainly winters in the Mediterranean region, also Africa south to the Equator, and sometimes as far south as South Africa. Commoner in west Africa than east Africa. Also occurs eastwards to northern Pakistan, south-east India, Sri-Lanka, Burma, southern China and Japan.

Movements Noted in Britain on spring and autumn passage, particularly in autumn on the south and east coasts. In autumn most birds are juveniles, often occurring well into October. In recent years up to 200 individuals have wintered in Britain, mainly along the south coast of England.

RECORD OF SIGHTINGS	
Date _____	Date _____
Place _____	Place _____
Male(s) _____ Female(s) _____	Male(s) _____ Female(s) _____
Immature _____ Eclipse _____	Immature _____ Eclipse _____
Behaviour Notes	

Redshank

Tringa totanus   27–29cm

Nest	Normally hidden in deep grass, but can be a scrape in sand with only sparse marram grass as cover
Egg clutch	4
Egg colour	Whitish or creamy-buff, spotted, streaked and blotched with reddish-brown
Laid	April/May
Incubation	21–25 days
Fledging	28 days

Identification A noisy, usually unapproachable bird flying up at the first hint of danger, revealing conspicuous white rear edges to the dark wings, and white back and rump giving a very black and white appearance. On landing it noticeably holds wings raised above its back for a moment or so, showing a very white underwing. In summer the rich brown upperparts, head and neck are strongly streaked and speckled. In winter it loses its warm brown colouring and looks quite grey. At all times the long, reddish bill tipped with black, and the vermilion red legs are distinctive. The legs of young birds are quite yellowish, as are adults in winter.
Voice A musical 'tuhu' and triple 'tu-hu-hu'. Also has a single alarm note 'teuk'.
Habitat In breeding season is equally at home on sand dunes, saltings and coastal marshes, while inland, prefers marshes, grassy waterside meadows, margins of lakes and reservoirs. In winter mudflats and tidal estuaries are mostly frequented.

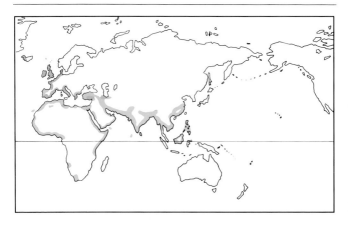

Food Molluscs, crustaceans and worms. At inland locations earthworms, cranefly larvae, vegetable matter, seeds and berries are also taken.

Range Breeds in Iceland, Britain and Ireland, Scandinavia and scattered inland areas of eastern Europe and eastward across Russia. Winters around coasts of Britain and Europe, also Mediterranean region and south to West Africa.

Movements In Britain birds return to their breeding grounds as early as January or February, though more typically March. In more northern climes it can be May before they arrive. By July nesting has been completed and birds begin their drift back to the coast and south to other wintering zones.

RECORD OF SIGHTINGS	
Date _____	Date _____
Place _____	Place _____
Male(s) _____ Female(s) _____	Male(s) _____ Female(s) _____
Immature _____ Eclipse _____	Immature _____ Eclipse _____
Behaviour Notes	

Greenshank

Tringa nebularia   30–34cm

Nest   A scrape, but sometimes quite a deep cup
Egg clutch 4
Egg colour Pale greenish, streaked and blotched or finely marked
                all over with reddish-brown
Laid   May
Incubation 25 days
Fledging   28 days

Identification In summer the dull grey upperparts are spotted,
streaked and blotched with black and brown, with head and neck
finely streaked. The underparts are white. The longish bill is
upturned, while the long legs are greenish, giving the bird its name.
In winter looks much paler, but at all times the extensive white V
up the back, as well as the dark wings and the call, help to identify
this bird. Though often probes and picks for food, quite frequently
sieves the ooze or chases small fish through the shallows. When
alarmed it will bob like the Redshank. On its breeding grounds it
will perch freely on stone walls, fences or rocks from where it will
often sing.
Voice A triple flutey 'tchu, tchu, tchu'.
Habitat Nests in swamps and marshes, clearings in the taiga, bogs
and on the tundra. At other times is found on marshes, along

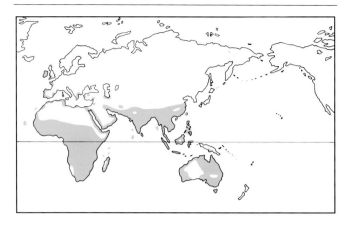

rivers, borders of lakes and reservoirs, salt marshes and estuaries.
Less frequently noted on the seashore.

Food Crustaceans, molluscs and other marine invertebrates, also
small fish and amphibians.

Range Breeds in Scotland eastwards across northern Europe
through Asia to the Kamchatka Peninsula.

Movements In spring birds return to their nesting grounds
throughout May and June. In autumn it is on the move by early
August, when Scandinavian birds and those that breed in the USSR
migrate south to winter beyond the Sahara. Up to 2000 individuals
winter in Britain and Ireland, most of which are to be found in
south-west Ireland.

RECORD OF SIGHTINGS	
Date _____	Date _____
Place _____	Place _____
Male(s) _____ Female(s) _____	Male(s) _____ Female(s) _____
Immature ____ Eclipse _____	Immature ____ Eclipse _____
Behaviour Notes	

Green Sandpiper
Tringa ochropus   21–24cm

Nest   Occupies disused nest of thrush, pigeon or crow
Egg clutch   4
Egg colour   Cream or olive, with dark streaks or blotches
Laid   May/June
Incubation   21 days
Fledging   28 days

Identification At a distance this medium-small stocky bird looks dark above and white below, but close views reveal a white eye-ring, a distinct white supercilium in front of the eye and fine olive-brown streaks on the chin and throat. These become denser on the breast and flanks, where they merge into blotches. The legs and bill are dark. In breeding plumage the upperparts have whitish spots but by August these have mostly gone. Juveniles are paler and browner-looking. Very distinctive in flight, with dark back and wings and a startlingly white rump.

Voice A loud ringing 'klu-weet-weeta-weeta' and a rippling 'tu-loo-ee'.

Habitat Forest swamps in breeding season, at other times a variety of shallow inland freshwater sites, with a marked aversion for coastal or tidal habitats.

Food A variety of aquatic invertebrates, and sometimes small fish.

Range Breeds in Scandinavia and eastern Europe through to Siberia. Has bred in Britain. Main wintering areas are in Central Africa, the Mediterranean basin and from Turkey and Iran

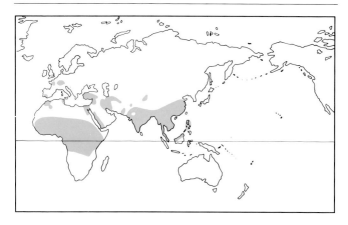

eastwards through India to China. However, some winter in more
temperate parts of western Europe, including Britain, where up to
1000 birds may be present, mainly scattered throughout south-east
England.

Movements The northwards movement through Europe peaks in
late April and May, though some birds are still passing through in
June. Migration occurs on a broad front, but numbers are small and
passage is swift. Females disperse early from the nesting grounds
and this species is one of the first migrants to head south again. By
the end of June, birds are noted moving through Britain. Most
occur in August, when small gatherings can be seen at favoured
sites. Concentrations of more than 50 are quite exceptional.

RECORD OF SIGHTINGS	
Date _____	Date _____
Place _____	Place _____
Male(s) _____ Female(s) _____	Male(s) _____ Female(s) _____
Immature _____ Eclipse _____	Immature _____ Eclipse _____
Behaviour Notes	

Wood Sandpiper

Tringa glareola   19–21cm

Nest   Scrape amongst dense cover, or occasionally old nest of Fieldfare, Waxwing, etc.
Egg clutch 4
Egg colour Pale green with dark markings
Laid   June
Incubation 21 days
Fledging   28 days

Identification Breeding adults have grey-brown upperparts, which are boldly speckled white, and white underparts, save for some brown streaking on the neck and breast. In winter plumage the upperparts are less clearly speckled, and the breast is greyish with much finer streaking. Juveniles are warmer brown above, with buff spots and fine brown streaks on the breast, which is initially washed buff but fades to white by late autumn. At all ages and seasons the white eyebrow is prominent. Confusion is most likely with the Green Sandpiper, but the Wood Sandpiper is smaller, slimmer and longer-legged (these are yellowish). In flight it looks more slender, the legs project well beyond the tail and it shows much less contrast between the dark wings and white rump than a Green Sandpiper.
Voice A characteristic 'chiff-if' or 'chiff, iff-iff'.
Habitat In breeding season damp conifer or birch woods, boggy moorland or marshes are chosen; at other times marshy areas and muddy margins of freshwater lakes and pools.
Food Freshwater and terrestrial insects, particularly beetles.
Range Breeds from Scandinavia across northern Russia, and

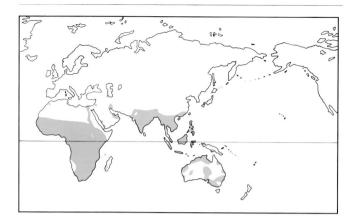

sporadically into the Aleutian Islands and Alaska. Nests sparingly in Scotland, with about half a dozen pairs at several scattered localities. Most winter in Africa but, exceptionally, a few remain as far north as Britain outside the breeding season. Has occurred as a vagrant along the eastern seaboard of the USA.

Movements Birds move northwards through Europe during April and May but seldom linger long in any one place. By end of May, most have reached breeding territories. Birds leave nesting grounds early, and by late June, some adults are on the move. Juveniles follow a month later and passage through western Europe peaks in late July and early August. A few stragglers are still around in October.

RECORD OF SIGHTINGS	
Date _____	Date _____
Place _____	Place _____
Male(s) _____ Female(s) _____	Male(s) _____ Female(s) _____
Immature _____ Eclipse _____	Immature _____ Eclipse _____
Behaviour Notes	

Common Sandpiper
Actitus hypoleucos 19–21cm

Nest A depression lined with grass, moss and leaves, usually in thick vegetation

Egg clutch 4

Egg colour Whitish to yellowish-brown, spotted, streaked and blotched red-brown

Laid May

Incubation 21–23 days

Fledging 28 days

Identification Easily distinguished from similar small sandpipers (except the Spotted Sandpiper) by the continual bobbing motion of its tail end, which is most obvious when it walks or perches on rock or boulder. The upperparts are brown, with patches on the side of the upper breast. There is a white 'peak' between the breast patch and the folded wing area, and the underparts are white. There is a shortish, straight bill and the short legs are usually a pale greyish colour. The flight, usually a foot or so above the water, consists of a regular, peculiar flickering wingbeat and momentary glide on down-curved wings, unique to the species. When disturbed, it often flies out over the water, returning to the shore in a wide arc, landing 40 metres or so from its starting point. There is a well-defined wing bar and white either side of the tail. The sexes are similar. In autumn juveniles are quite heavily barred on the wing coverts.

Voice A far-carrying 'dee-dee-dee-dee'. On breeding grounds song is 'kitti-wee-wit, kitti-wee-wit', uttered in flight or on ground.

Habitat In breeding season favours fast-running streams or borders of lakes, lochs and tarns, usually in or close to hilly country. Occasionally chooses more lowland areas. Outside breeding season, found along rivers, streams, margins of reservoirs, sand and gravel

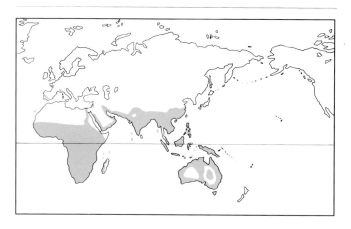

workings. Also occurs along river estuaries but rarely on open mudflats.

Food Insects, worms, small molluscs and crustaceans.

Range Breeds extensively in most parts of Britain and Europe eastwards through Asia to China and Japan. European birds winter south of the Sahara, while those of Asian origin move to India, south-east Asia, and some reach Australia.

Movements Some birds are on the move in March but main passage is late April or early May. Returns south after nesting, often as early as July. Main movement in August but noted well into September and even October. About 100 individuals winter in the southern half of Britain every year.

RECORD OF SIGHTINGS	
Date _____	Date _____
Place _____	Place _____
Male(s) _____ Female(s) _____	Male(s) _____ Female(s) _____
Immature _____ Eclipse _____	Immature _____ Eclipse _____
Behaviour Notes	

Turnstone

Arenaria interpres   21–25cm

Nest	A shallow cup on well-vegetated rocky or gravelly ground
Egg clutch	4
Egg colour	Glossy brownish or olive green, with some grey mottling and black spots
Laid	June
Incubation	24 days
Fledging	24–26 days

Identification In summer plumage both sexes have a pied head and upper breast, forming a strong facial pattern and black chest band. The male has a whiter crown at this stage. The mantle and wings are predominantly chestnut with bands of black. The lower breast and belly are pure white. In flight shows a white stripe down the centre of the back and a pair of white shoulder stripes. There is a white wing bar and a white tail with a black sub-terminal band, giving the bird an unmistakable pattern. The legs are orange-red and the short beak is black. In winter the head, back and coverts are brown but the basic design of the plumage is essentially the same. At all times the distinctive feeding behaviour of flicking over shoreline debris and turning shells and stones over to get at food gives the bird its name. Juveniles are dark brown above with a white throat, dark breast band and white below; legs are orange-red.

Voice A rapid, staccato 'trik-tuc-tuc-tuc' call.

Habitat In breeding season chooses rocky coastal islands and more elevated Arctic tundra. In winter prefers rocky seaweed-covered rocks, pebbly beaches and, to a lesser extent, muddy and sandy areas.

Food On the breeding grounds mainly plant material, but also larval insects and other invertebrates; at other times sandhoppers,

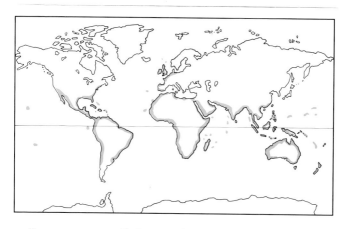

molluscs, crustaceans, fly larvae and suchlike.

Range Breeding area spans the Arctic from Alaska to Siberia, penetrating as far south as Sweden. In the winter to be found around the coasts of all the warm continents. A substantial number remain on the Atlantic fringe of western Europe.

Movements A hardy long-distance traveller to be found on beaches throughout the world. In spring moves north to reach breeding grounds late May to early June, returning southwards from end of July onwards. Passes northwards through Britain in May, when birds are often encountered at inland waters. In winter around 50,000 birds are to be found at suitable feeding localities around the coast.

RECORD OF SIGHTINGS	
Date _____	Date _____
Place _____	Place _____
Male(s) _____ Female(s) _____	Male(s) _____ Female(s) _____
Immature ____ Eclipse _____	Immature ____ Eclipse _____
Behaviour Notes	

Red-necked Phalarope
Phalaropus lobatus   18–19cm

Nest   A scrape lined with leaves and grass stems
Egg clutch 4
Egg colour Buffy-olive, blotched with dark brown
Laid   June
Incubation 21 days
Fledging   About 21 days

Identification The size of a Dunlin, this is the smallest of the
phalaropes, with a slim neck, small oval head and long, needle-fine
bill, giving it an overall slender and elegant appearance. The
breeding female has a slate-grey head, neck and back, with buff
edgings to the scapulars and mantle, brownish wings, a white throat
and belly and a grey breast band. The most distinctive feature,
however, is the orange-red horseshoe mark on the neck. The male is
similarly patterned but much duller and more diffuse, with browner
upperparts, a paler orange neck and a less distinctive neck band.
Winter adults can easily be confused with Grey/Red Phalaropes.
Juveniles can be distinguished by a brownish-black cap and dark
brown upperparts, with buff margins to the mantle and scapulars.
Their white underparts have a buffish suffusion.
Voice A 'whit' or 'prip', similar to Grey Phalarope but
lower-pitched.
Habitat Breeds around coasts and near inland pools, particularly
where there is emergent vegetation. Marshy ground with tiny pools
and watercourses set among rich lowland vegetation is also
favoured. On migration will stop off and feed on any lake or pool,
no matter how small. At other times found on sea shore and way
out on the oceans.
Food On the breeding ground eats chironomid midges especially,

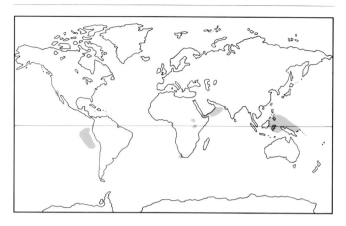

plus other small insects and their larvae. Its most characteristic
means of taking such food is from the water's surface while
'spinning'.

Range Breeds right across the Holarctic region but winters in
warmer latitudes, principally off Peru, in the Arabian Sea and
around the East Indies. Small numbers breed in the Outer Hebrides
and the Northern Isles.

Movements Northwards migration is late, occurring between
April and early June. Almost immediately after the eggs hatch,
some females begin their return south, unless they take up with
another male and lay a second clutch. Males start their journey
south in July. The young follow in August and early September.

RECORD OF SIGHTINGS	
Date _____	Date _____
Place _____	Place _____
Male(s) _____ Female(s) _____	Male(s) _____ Female(s) _____
Immature _____ Eclipse _____	Immature _____ Eclipse _____
Behaviour Notes	

Grey Phalarope
Phalaropus fulicarius 20–22cm

Nest   A shallow cup lined with any available material
Egg clutch 4
Egg colour Olive, with dark spots and blotches
Laid   June
Incubation 21 days
Fledging   14–15 days

Identification Quite unmistakable in breeding plumage, having
prominent white cheeks, rich chestnut underparts, blackish-brown
back with pale buff feather edgings and a black-tipped yellow bill.
Females can have an unstreaked black-brown chin, crown and
hindneck. The males are similar but duller and more mottled. They
have streaking on the crown, dingier cheeks and drabber
underparts, often with some white on the belly. However, the
plumage differences between breeding males and females is less
marked than in the other two species of phalaropes. The short-lived
juvenile plumage suggests a washed-out adult. In winter the
plumage is basically white, except for a blackish-grey crown that
extends some way on the hindneck, a pale grey back and a blackish
mark through and behind the eye. The bill is thicker and broader,
the head is bigger and the neck is thicker than in the Red-necked
Phalarope. On the water it swims with its back horizontal and the
tail held higher. In flight shows longer, broader wings than Red-
necked, though wing bars are less obvious than in that species.

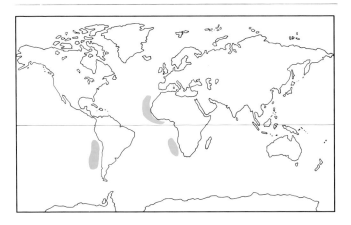

Voice Usual call is a whistling 'wit'.

Habitat In breeding season prefers marshy tundra that surrounds Arctic coasts and islands, usually where there are pools with muddy shorelines. In winter almost entirely oceanic.

Food Insect larvae, crustaceans, insects, vegetable matter and seeds. Out at sea various planktonic fare.

Range Breeds discontinuously around the Arctic Circle. Main wintering grounds are off the coasts of West and South Africa and Chile. Some birds remain as far north as the North Sea.

Movements Most frequently noted in western Europe and in Britain after autumn gales in September and October. Occasionally occurs inland, but usually juveniles.

RECORD OF SIGHTINGS	
Date _____	Date _____
Place _____	Place _____
Male(s) _____ Female(s) _____	Male(s) _____ Female(s) _____
Immature _____ Eclipse _____	Immature _____ Eclipse _____
Behaviour Notes	

RARE MIGRANTS AND VAGRANTS

Semipalmated Plover
Charadrius semipalmatus   17–19cm

Identification A small, compact, rotund plover. Adults in
breeding plumage have a white forehead, above which is a black
fore-crown that meets the lower black facial line around the eye.
The dark eye has a slim yellow orbital ring. Behind the eye the
black ear coverts fade to light brown, which meets with the light
brown of the crown and nape. There is a full white collar and
below this is a full black breast band. The underparts are white.
The short stubby bill is orange with a black tip and the legs and
feet are yellowish orange. At all ages has a greater amount of
webbing between the three toes, giving rise to the bird's common
name. In flight there is a slim yet obvious wing bar.

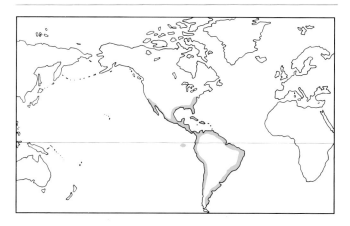

Voice A sharp 'chuwit'.

Habitat Nests on open flat areas of tundra and gravel plains. In winter haunts wide sandy or muddy beaches and coastal lagoons.

Food Molluscs, worms and insects taken in typical plover fashion.

Range Breeding area extends from Alaska across the whole of northern Canada to Newfoundland.

Movements After nesting many move to the more southerly coasts of the USA. Others continue south to central and South America. An extremely rare visitor to Britain. To date there is only one accepted occurrence of this species — a juvenile identified on St Agnes, Isles of Scilly, from 9 October to at least 9 November, 1978.

RECORD OF SIGHTINGS	
Date _____	Date _____
Place _____	Place _____
Male(s) _____ Female(s) _____	Male(s) _____ Female(s) _____
Immature ____ Eclipse _____	Immature ____ Eclipse _____
Behaviour Notes	

Killdeer
Charadrius vociferus   23–26cm

Identification The only shorebird in North America with a double black breast band, which contrasts with the rest of its underparts, which are clean white. The head appears quite large, set on a fairly short and thick neck, showing a black and white face pattern with a brownish head-crown. The upperparts are dark brown but when the bird takes flight, a bright orange-rufous rump and upper tail is revealed. The remainder of the tail is dark brown and narrowly edged with white. Also in flight, a conspicuous white wing bar is to be seen. The legs are dull, yellowish-grey, while the bright orange-red eye ring gives the bird a deceptively gentle appearance.

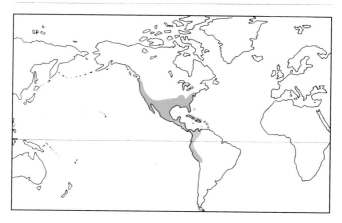

Voice A loud penetrating 'kill-dee' or 'kill-deah', from which the bird gets it name.

Habitat Can be found from seashore up to land above 2500 metres. Favours short grassy areas and bare ground, such as meadows and arable fields. Often found close to human habitation on gravel tracks, lawns and golf courses.

Food Wide variety of insect food, plus worms and other invertebrates, taken in typical plover fashion. Also follows plough in search of unearthed larvae and worms.

Range Breeds widely across North America.

Movements A rare migrant Britain, one or two occurring in most years.

RECORD OF SIGHTINGS	
Date _____	Date _____
Place _____	Place _____
Male(s) _____ Female(s) _____	Male(s) _____ Female(s) _____
Immature _____ Eclipse _____	Immature _____ Eclipse _____
Behaviour Notes	

American Golden Plover
Pluvialis dominica   23–26cm

Identification In summer plumage a very smart-looking bird with
jet-black face; throat, centre of chest, belly and undertail coverts
form a continuous and solidly dark underside. The black face
extends just over the bill and above this the prominent white
forehead extends with a thick eyebrow. The white blaze envelops
the rear ear coverts, then continues to broaden at the sides of the
neck to form an oval patch flanking the black of the chest. The
upperparts are a mixture of small black, golden and white feathers,
giving a spangled effect. In flight the dusky grey underwing and
axillaries are a useful field mark. In winter a uniform-looking bird.
Voice Regularly used contact calls are a 'chu-wit' and a 'tu-ee'.
Habitat A true tundra bird, preferring dry gentle slopes with short
vegetation for nesting. In winter inhabits short grassland and tilled

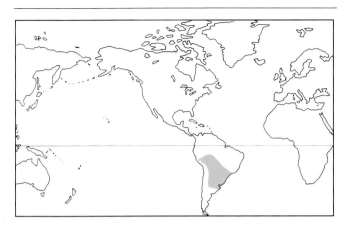

agricultural fields, but at times haunts coastal lagoons, mudflats and inland shallow pools.

Food Invertebrates on breeding grounds, but berries and other vegetable matter taken. Insects and worms are a major food source at other times.

Range Nesting area extends from western Alaska to Baffin Island.

Movements The Atlantic loop flight-path, as it is often known, makes this and other American waders susceptible to bad weather displacement. Following hurricane-force winds in the North Atlantic at migration times, it is not unusual for American Golden Plovers to turn up in the British Isles. Though a rare visitor, one or two – sometimes more – are recorded in most years.

RECORD OF SIGHTINGS	
Date _____	Date _____
Place _____	Place _____
Male(s) _____ Female(s) _____	Male(s) ____ Female(s) _____
Immature ____ Eclipse _____	Immature ____ Eclipse _____
Behaviour Notes	

Pacific Golden Plover
Pluvialis fulva   23–26cm

Identification Until recently this bird and the American Golden Plover were treated as a single species named the Lesser or American Golden Plover. In breeding plumage both Pacific and American Golden Plovers have predominantly black underparts, but the Pacific has a narrow white line all the way along its flanks from the eyebrow to the undertail, usually broken by black bars on the flanks. Importantly, the Pacific also has largely white undertail coverts. The upperparts are generally more distinctly golden-spangled. In winter the Pacific is essentially yellowish-buff with bright yellow spangles on the upperparts and a brownish-buff breast (buffish in juveniles), mottled bright yellow in both.
Voice A plaintive 'ki-wee' and a 'chewit' note reminiscent of a subdued Spotted Redshank's call.
Habitat On breeding territory favours well-drained tundra beyond the tree-line with short sward, moss and lichen. In winter largely coastal, haunting inter-tidal mud and beaches. Also likes areas of short grass, such as golf courses, playing fields and salt marshes.
Food A variety of small invertebrates supplemented by berries in the autumn.

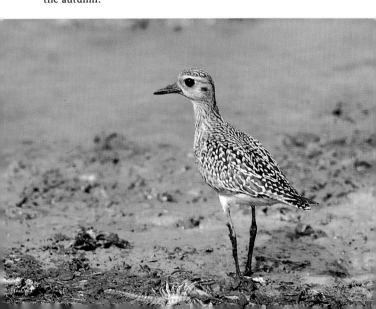

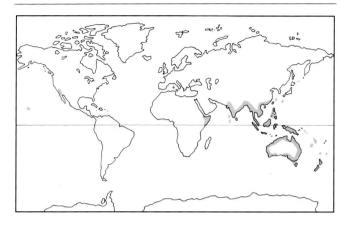

Range Arctic Siberia from Yamal peninsula eastward. Also western Alaska and the Bering Sea islands. Winters from north-east Africa around shores of Indian Ocean to south-east Asia, and south to Australia and New Zealand. Birds also reach Pacific Islands. A few are found in southern California.

Movements A prodigious migrant, often travelling enormous distances, for example 4500 km from Pribilov Islands in Bering Sea to Hawaii. Adults leave breeding grounds July onwards, several weeks before juveniles. Return journey starts as early as March, but many juveniles spend first summer in winter quarters. Has been recorded in Western Europe, but to date only four have appeared in Britain, all since 1976.

RECORD OF SIGHTINGS	
Date _____	Date _____
Place _____	Place _____
Male(s) _____ Female(s) _____	Male(s) _____ Female(s) _____
Immature _____ Eclipse _____	Immature _____ Eclipse _____
Behaviour Notes	

Semipalmated Sandpiper
Calidris pusilla 13–15cm

Identification In summer plumage a rather dull-looking bird with the upperparts a mixture of black, buff and grey. The underparts are white, while there is an extensive streaked breast band. The dark bill is short and straight with a deep base. It is blunt-tipped in profile and in good head-on views usually shows a slight expansion of the tip. The legs are blackish. In flight a narrow whitish wing bar and white sides to rump and tail can be seen. In winter plumage there is no extensive streaking on the breast or darker marking on the upperparts.

Voice A harsh low pitched 'churk' or 'chrup'. Sometimes utters a 'chirrup' reminiscent of a Pectoral Sandpiper. On breeding ground has a monotonous trilling 'pee pee see' or 'di-jip di-jip' uttered in a trilling aerial display.

Habitat Wet coastal and low inland tundra for nesting. Wintering in large flocks on estuary mudflats.

Food Insects and inter-tidal invertebrates.

Range Breeds from mouth of the River Yukon on the west coast of Alaska east to Victoria Island, around Hudson Bay on to Baffin Island and Labrador. Winters on Pacific coast of Central America, north to Guatemala, in the West Indies, and in coastal South

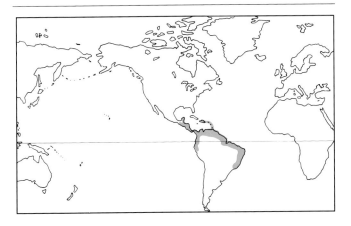

America to Peru and Uruguay.

Movements Birds from different breeding areas take different migratory routes south across North America: Alaskan birds pass through the Great Plains; the central Canadian population moves south-east; eastern birds move via the Gulf of St Lawrence across the Atlantic direct to the Caribbean. In spring the central Canadian population joins Alaskan birds on migration through the Great Plains, while east Canadian birds follow the Atlantic coast northwards. Before 1980 there were only ten records of vagrants in Britain. From that time until 1986 another 38 individuals have been successfully identified. Most of these have been noted in Ireland and south-west England.

RECORD OF SIGHTINGS	
Date _____	Date _____
Place _____	Place _____
Male(s) _____ Female(s) _____	Male(s) _____ Female(s) _____
Immature _____ Eclipse _____	Immature _____ Eclipse _____
Behaviour Notes	

Western Sandpiper
Calidris mauri   14–17cm

Identification Often difficult to distinguish from Semipalmated Sandpiper, but in breeding plumage points of difference are rusty-orange centres to upper scapulars and rufous patch on crown and ear coverts, contrasting with grey wing coverts, nape and mantle. The breast is heavily marked with dark streaks, often extending as a distinctive line of chevrons along the flanks. The black bill, of variable length, usually has a slightly decurved drooped tip. The legs are also black. In winter plumage it is almost identical to the Semipalmated Sandpiper. However, juvenile Western Sandpipers are relatively distinct, being less scaly and less uniform, also paler faced with less defined supercilium and dark eyestripe.
Voice On the breeding ground the song is a series of ascending notes followed by a buzzing trill. The typical call is a thin squeaky 'jeet' or 'cheep'.
Habitat Well-drained tundra from sea level to the lower slopes of

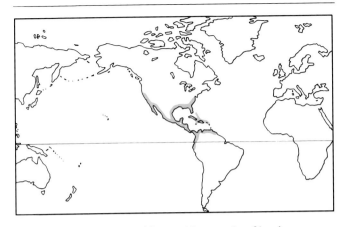

the mountains, preferring ridges and hummocks of heath
interspersed with low-lying small pools and lakes for nesting.
During winter haunts open mudflats.

Food Mostly insects, especially flies.

Range As a breeding bird, confined to northern and western
Alaska and the east coast of the Chukotskiy peninsula in extreme
eastern Siberia. In winter found along the Pacific coast from
California south to Peru, on the Gulf of Mexico, on the Atlantic
coast north to New England, in the Caribbean, and on the Atlantic
coast of South America east to Surinam. A vagrant to Japan,
Australia and western Europe, with only six records for Britain and
Ireland up to 1988.

RECORD OF SIGHTINGS	
Date _____	Date _____
Place _____	Place _____
Male(s) _____ Female(s) _____	Male(s) _____ Female(s) _____
Immature _____ Eclipse _____	Immature _____ Eclipse _____
Behaviour Notes	

Least Sandpiper
Calidris minutilla   13–15cm

Identification Marginally the smallest shorebird in the world. In breeding plumage looks dark brown at a distance with dingy, well-streaked head and breast. Closer inspection reveals a fine pale V at the side of the mantle and a rusty tone to the crown and ear coverts and upperparts. The underparts are white. The bill is short and fine, curving gradually throughout its full length. Legs are pale yellowish, greenish or brownish. Winter plumage looks dark brownish-grey with the dark centres of the feathers on the upperparts producing a slightly blotchy effect. There is a neat dusky breast and quite a prominent pale supercilium. The juvenile looks quite bright and may recall the Little Stint or a tiny Pectoral Sandpiper in its general plumage pattern. In flight it shows a white wing bar and white sides to the rump.

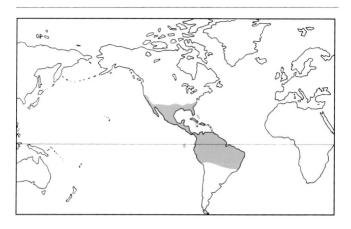

Voice A shrill high rolling 'kreeep' or disyllabic 'kre-ep', as well as a lower pitched vibrant 'prrrt'.

Habitat Marshy areas within spruce forests, sedge meadows, flat sandy islands and boggy tundra for nesting. In winter less coastal, occurring in upper reaches of salt-marshes as well as inland on the margins of fresh water and in wet grazing meadows.

Food Small insects, flies, larvae and tiny marine invertebrates.

Range Breeds in western Alaska through northern Canada, south to north-west British Columbia, northern Ontario, Nova Scotia and east to Southampton Island and northern Labrador. Winters in the Gulf of Mexico, the Caribbean and west South America. A vagrant to Japan and western Europe, and a less than annual visitor to Britain.

RECORD OF SIGHTINGS	
Date _____	Date _____
Place _____	Place _____
Male(s) _____ Female(s) _____	Male(s) _____ Female(s) _____
Immature ____ Eclipse _____	Immature ____ Eclipse _____
Behaviour Notes	

White-rumped Sandpiper

Calidris fusicollis   15–18cm

Identification In breeding plumage is mottled with buff, grey and black on the upperparts and a rusty tinge to the crown, ear coverts and scapulars. The throat and breast are streaked and spotted with black, the streaks becoming larger black Vs on the flanks. The underparts are white. The short straight bill is blackish, often with a dull green or yellowish base. The legs are black. In flight shows a narrow white wing bar. The white 'rump' is, in fact, a white band on the upper tail. In winter is dun-grey above and shows a prominent white supercilium. The breast is washed grey with finer dark markings. The juvenile is scaly above and has prominent splashes of chestnut on the fringes of the back and crown feathers. There is a white 'brace' on the sides of the mantle and a contrastingly grey hindneck and breast. The latter is well streaked and a few of the streaks extend to the flanks. A white supercilium sets off a chestnut cap.

Voice A strange, quiet, high-pitched squeak, a 'jeet' often given in a couplet and likened to the squeak of a mouse.

Habitat Wet lowland and upland tundra with plenty of grassy tussocks and hummocks, near a river, lake or group of pools is the usual nesting requirement. In winter frequents lake shores, wet pastures and sea beaches, brackish swamps and especially mudflats, where it can be found in large numbers.

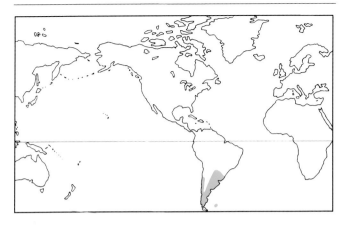

Food Tiny molluscs, insects, small worms and seeds on breeding grounds.

Range Arctic Canada from northern Mackenzie to southern Baffin Island, occasionally northern Alaska. Winters South America mainly east of the Andes and south of the Equator, mostly from southern Brazil to Tierra del Fuego and the Falkland Islands. Spring passage northwards is more westerly than in the autumn, overflying the Great Antilles and Gulf of Mexico and across the Great Plains.

Movements A vagrant to western Europe, but recorded annually in Britain in autumn. Up to 1986, recorded on 293 occasions, with as many as 29 noted in 1984.

RECORD OF SIGHTINGS	
Date _____	Date _____
Place _____	Place _____
Male(s) _____ Female(s) _____	Male(s) _____ Female(s) _____
Immature _____ Eclipse _____	Immature _____ Eclipse _____
Behaviour Notes	

Baird's Sandpiper
Calidris bairdii   14–17cm

Identification Generally buffer-looking than White-rumped Sandpiper, it lacks the brighter tones of that species in breeding and juvenile plumage. However, always shows a neat, finely-streaked breast band and unstreaked flanks. There is a less well marked supercilium than the White-rumped Sandpiper. At all times the fine-tipped bill and legs are blackish. In summer adults are quite 'mealy' in appearance above, their plumage consisting of a mixture of buff, black and grey, with large black centres to the central scapulars. In winter they are grey-brown above with fine pale scaling only obvious at close quarters. The juvenile is dull grey-brown with neat buff or whitish fringes to the upperparts, giving it a distinctive scaly appearance. The underparts are white in all plumages. In flight shows a narrow white wing bar and narrow white sides to tail.

Voice A low raspy trilling 'preeet' or 'kreeep'.

Habitat The favoured breeding situation is dry, elevated tundra among dunes or saltwater lagoons, but sometimes chooses mountain-sides well away from coast. At other times, freshwater margins and damp fields, as well as dry areas of short cropland and

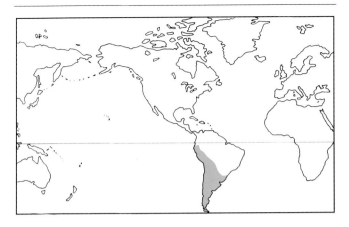

pasture up to 4000 metres above sea level. When found on coast, prefers upper reaches of beach.

Food All manner of small invertebrates, plus insects and spiders.

Range The high Arctic from Chukotskiy peninsula in north-east Siberia across northern Alaska and Canada, east to Baffin Island and north-west Greenland. Wintering area is South America, south of the Equator from the high Andes in southern Ecuador, south to Tierra del Fuego.

Movements The species is a vagrant to Hawaii, the Galapagos, Australia, New Zealand, Japan, Siskhalin and the Furile Islands, and in the east to South Africa, Senegal and Western Europe. A vagrant to Britain, it has occurred annually since 1969 with an average of six records a year in the past decade.

RECORD OF SIGHTINGS	
Date _____	Date _____
Place _____	Place _____
Male(s) _____ Female(s) _____	Male(s) _____ Female(s) _____
Immature _____ Eclipse _____	Immature _____ Eclipse _____
Behaviour Notes	

Broad-billed Sandpiper
Limicola falcinellus   16–18cm

Identification Slightly smaller than a Dunlin, shows a double
supercilium splitting just in front of the eye, with the upper fork
weaker and less well-marked. There is also a prominent dark
eyestripe. In breeding plumage appears dark with a well-defined
breast band of arrowheads and streaks extending on to the flanks.
The upperparts are well striped and the feathering forms two white
Vs on the sides of the mantle and scapulars. In winter looks grey
above with fine pale scaling and some dark feather centres, giving a
mottled effect. There is a darker area in the bend of the wing. The
upper supercilium may be faint and difficult to see. Juveniles
resemble breeding adults, but have breast washed with buff and
finely speckled. There are no streaks on the flanks, resulting in a
neat pectoral band. In flight shows white sides to tail and a narrow
white wing bar. The black bill is long with a distinct downward
kink near the tip. The legs are short and dark.
Voice A dry buzzing trill-like 'chrreet'.
Habitat Breeding area comprises both lowland and mountain
marshy tundra, often in boggy areas with adjacent swampy
meadows surrounded by coniferous forests. At other times muddy
vegetated freshwater margins or salt marshes are frequented.

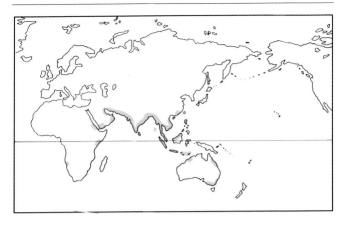

(Siberian population found on open shores and mudflats.)

Food Marine and freshwater invertebrates, and at times seeds.

Range Breeds in south central Norway, central and southern Sweden, northern Finland and adjacent areas of the USSR. (There is another population found in three widely separated areas of northern Siberia which winters around the shores of the Indian Ocean.)

Movements Autumn passage spans the period July to end of October, but wintering area is not fully known. They move southeast across Europe and the Middle East. Occurrences in a westward direction are increasing and recorded more frequently in Britain in recent years.

RECORD OF SIGHTINGS	
Date _____	Date _____
Place _____	Place _____
Male(s) _____ Female(s) _____	Male(s) _____ Female(s) _____
Immature _____ Eclipse _____	Immature _____ Eclipse _____
Behaviour Notes	

Stilt Sandpiper
Micropalama himantopus 18–21cm

Identification Non-breeding birds look mainly greyish at a
distance but closer views reveal white fringes to the feathers on
upperparts and a distinct white supercilium, contrasting with
darker lores and crown. The underparts are whitish with fine
darker grey streaking on the breast and flanks. From March birds
moult into distinctive breeding dress, with a dark barred lower
breast and belly and dark streaked neck. The black feathers of the
upperparts show rufous and white borders. The white supercilium
is even more conspicuous, contrasting strongly with a darker
crown, warm chestnut lores, ear coverts and nape. The legs are
rather long, as the name suggests, and these are ochre-yellow. The
longish bill is marginally thicker and only slightly decurved
compared with the Curlew Sandpiper. In flight shows little trace of
a wing bar, the grey-brown of the wing contrasting with the whole
upper tail coverts, which are square cut in line with the trailing
edge of the wings. Juveniles resemble winter adults but show a
darker crown and more prominent white supercilium.
Voice A soft trilled 'krrr' or 'srrrt'.
Habitat Mainly dry tundra for nesting, but at other times shows a

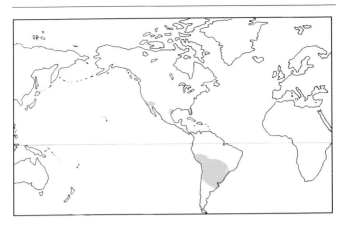

clear preference for shallow grassy pools, flooded marshes and the shores of ponds and lakes. Less frequently on hard sandy beaches and tidal mudflats.

Food Mainly adult and larval beetles, small molluscs and larval insects, with probably a few seeds and berries also taken.

Range Breeds in northern Alaska to north-eastern Ontario. Some winter in the southern United States, Mexico and the Caribbean, but most spend non-breeding season in central South America.

Movements First recorded in the British Isles in 1954 but remains a true vagrant with no more than 17 officially accepted occurrences up to 1986. After the first record there were seven during the 1960s, five in the 1970s and four between 1983 and 1985.

RECORD OF SIGHTINGS	
Date _____	Date _____
Place _____	Place _____
Male(s) _____ Female(s) _____	Male(s) _____ Female(s) _____
Immature ____ Eclipse _____	Immature ____ Eclipse _____
Behaviour Notes	

Buff-breasted Sandpiper
Tryngites subruficollis   18–20cm

Identification Adult birds have a fairly bright apricot/buff-coloured face and underparts that are unmarked apart from a few darker spots at the sides of the breast. The crown is flecked darker giving a capped effect at times, while the remainder of the upperparts is grey or black with buff fringes. The bill is generally dark and the legs a fairly bright yellow ochre. The small black eye surrounded by a paler orbital ring stands out in an otherwise plain-looking face that gives the bird a rather docile expression. The male birds are up to 10 per cent larger than females. In flight appears fairly long-winged, which is noticeably white underneath. Juveniles are like adults but have paler broad fringes to the feathers, looking more scaly on the upperparts.

Voice A 'prreet' alarm call.

Habitat Breeds on the drier slopes of grass or lichen tundra. At other times haunts dry, open grassland, and on migration will visit golf courses, airfields and stubble fields.

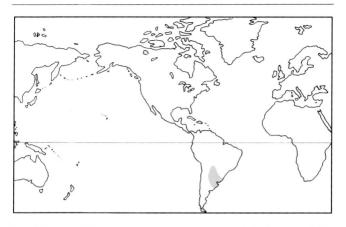

Food Terrestrial insects and invertebrates, especially beetle and fly larvae.

Range Breeds in northern Alaska to western Canada, with a few pairs in eastern Siberia. Winters on the Argentinian and Paraguayan pampas.

Movements A vagrant to the British Isles, and the second most numerous American wader to cross the Atlantic. Since 1967 it has been an annual visitor to the Isles of Scilly, usually to be seen on the airfield or golf course. In some years more than 60 individuals have been recorded in Britain. There has been some evidence of a decline in recent years, and for the first time in two decades, none were noted on the Isles of Scilly in 1986.

RECORD OF SIGHTINGS	
Date _____	Date _____
Place _____	Place _____
Male(s) _____ Female(s) _____	Male(s) _____ Female(s) _____
Immature ____ Eclipse _____	Immature ____ Eclipse _____
Behaviour Notes	

Short-billed Dowitcher

Limnodromus griseus   25–29cm

Identification A medium-sized, stocky shorebird with long snipe-like bill and relatively short legs. Feeds on open mud or shallow water with head down in distinctive sewing machine-like action. In breeding plumage it is rusty orange-red below and a mixture of black, buff and rufous above. Some have a white belly, a feature never shown by the Long-billed Dowitcher in summer plumage. In flight has a distinctive shape, with a plump body and comparatively narrow wings, as well as long, straight bill. There is a lozenge-shaped white wedge on the rump and lower back and the tail is barred dark and white, appearing great at a distance. In winter looks dull grey above and white below, washed grey on breast and flanks, with a distinct white supercilium. Juveniles have underparts and head washed with buff, and the feathers of the crown and upperparts have broad orange-buff fringes and irregular orange markings within dark centres, notably on 'tiger-striped' tertials.

Voice A mellow 'tu-tu-tu', recalling a Lesser Yellowlegs.

Habitat Swamps and open marshes, quaking bogs with low scrub, and sometimes swampy coastal tundra are used for nesting. At other times can be found in a wide variety of wetlands inland and along the coast.

Food Various marine invertebrates, earthworms, flies and their larvae; also seeds of aquatic plants.

Range Breeds in three distinct areas of northern North America: eastern Canada (northern Quebec), northern Canada (eastern British Columbia, northern Alberta, Saskatchewan and Manitoba)

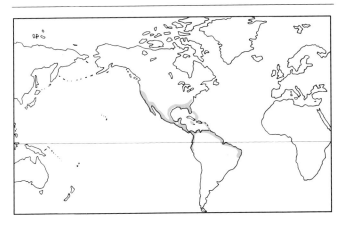

and southern Alaska. Breeding Alaskan birds winter on the coast from California south to Peru (some more inland in the western States). Central Canadian birds winter on the Gulf coast and both east and west coasts of Central America as far south as Panama; some move to the Atlantic coast from Long Island southwards. Those from Quebec winter from North Carolina to Florida and around the shores of the Caribbean and South America to Brazil.

Movements An extremely rare visitor to the British Isles. There are only five currently accepted records, including some doubtful late nineteenth-century records. The most recent and most certain was in County Wexford, Ireland, between 30 September and 2 October, 1985.

RECORD OF SIGHTINGS	
Date _____	Date _____
Place _____	Place _____
Male(s) _____ Female(s) _____	Male(s) _____ Female(s) _____
Immature _____ Eclipse _____	Immature _____ Eclipse _____
Behaviour Notes	

Long-billed Dowitcher
Limnodromus scolopaceus   27–30cm

Identification Very similar in appearance to the Short-billed Dowitcher, it has a rather different breeding distribution and is a more regular transatlantic vagrant. In summer plumage the orangy-red is a much deeper shade, while the foreneck is spotted brown and the breast is spotted and barred — otherwise similar and requires ideal viewing conditions to ascertain the more subtle differences (see Short-billed Dowitcher). However the juvenile plumages of the two can be readily distinguished, as Long-billed Dowitchers are washed with buff below, often with a distinctly greyer head and neck, while the upperparts show narrow rusty fringes and solidly dark centres.

Voice The best distinguishing feature — a shrill, slightly Oystercatcher-like 'keek', sometimes in an excited series when alarmed.

Habitat Breeding area is tundra beyond the tree-line in grassy or sedgy swamps, often near a small lake. At other times prefers freshwater or brackish pools to inter-tidal mud, though frequently makes use of the latter.

Food Various freshwater molluscs, earthworms, flies and their larvae; also marine invertebrates and seeds.

Range Breeds along the north-east coast of Siberia from the Chukotskiy peninsula west to Van Karem Bay and in the Anadyr

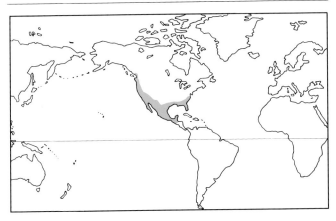

basin. In North America breeds on St Lawrence Island and coastal and western Alaska, and probably north-west Mackenzie and the northern Yukon. Wintering grounds in southern USA extend from South Carolina and Florida west to central California and then south through Mexico to Panama. A rare but regular migrant in Japan; a vagrant to Bali, Brunei, Thailand and western Europe.

Movements Its autumn migration route takes it on a great circle over the North Atlantic and down the eastern seaboard of the USA at a time when autumn storms make it more susceptible to transatlantic displacement. It is the fourth most commonly recorded American wader in the British Isles. In the last decade an average of ten a year has been recorded.

RECORD OF SIGHTINGS	
Date _____	Date _____
Place _____	Place _____
Male(s) _____ Female(s) _____	Male(s) _____ Female(s) _____
Immature _____ Eclipse _____	Immature _____ Eclipse _____
Behaviour Notes	

Hudsonian Godwit

Limosa haemastica   35–40cm

Identification In breeding plumage has deep chestnut red-brown and red belly, light grey head and neck which contrast markedly with the black and yellow-spangled back, giving the bird a very regal look. The long orange bill with a black tip is slightly upturned, while the longish legs are dark grey. Normally shy and easily disturbed, it takes flight, revealing narrow white wing bars, a black and white tail and protruding legs. At such times it bears some resemblance to the European Black-tailed Godwit, but is more slender-looking with less extensive areas of white on the wings and tail. In winter plumage, however, both species look similar, with greyish upperparts and a white breast underneath, but the Hudsonian Godwit has only to raise its wings, revealing the jet black linings, to dispel any doubt as to its identity.

Voice A modulating trill reminiscent of the Whimbrel.

Habitat For nesting chooses sedge marshes, bogs and meadows in the vicinity of lakes and coast at the edge of the tree-line. At other times chooses a variety of aquatic habitats, from estuaries and tidal

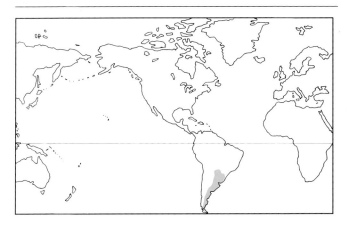

beaches to freshwater and saline lagoons.

Food Worms, molluscs and crustaceans.

Range Breeds in north-western British Columbia, parts of Alaska and northern Canada from the Mackenzie rift valley to Hudson Bay. Winters in Argentina south to Tierra del Fuego.

Movements A vagrant to Britain. The first record of this species was an adult with four Black-tailed Godwits on Blacktoft Sands, Humberside, from 10 September to 3 October, 1961. On 22 November the same year, what was presumably the same bird appeared at Countess Weir, Devonshire. It remained until mid-January, 1982. A year later a Hudsonian Godwit again appeared at Blacktoft Sands between 6 April and 26 May.

RECORD OF SIGHTINGS	
Date _____	Date _____
Place _____	Place _____
Male(s) _____ Female(s) _____	Male(s) _____ Female(s) _____
Immature ____ Eclipse _____	Immature ____ Eclipse _____
Behaviour Notes	

Upland Sandpiper
Batramia longicauda   28–32cm

Identification About the size of a Yellowlegs, its long tail projects beyond the wingtips when at rest, while a small head is supported by a neck which, when stretched, can look ridiculously thin. The short, straight bill has a darker ridge and tip. In general appearance recalls a small Curlew. Notably the crown is blackish, with an indistinct buffish crown stripe. Otherwise the face is plain but the eye is prominent and staring. In flight has a cross-like outline with long wings and tail. The centre of the back, rump and tail are particularly dark, as is the outer wing. From below the heavily barred underwing and axillaries are notable. Often flies with shallow fluttering wingbeats.
Voice The flight call is a liquid flutey 'quip-quip-ip' reminiscent of a quail. On nesting grounds a bubbling 'quip-ip-ip-ip-ip-ip-ip'.
Habitat For nesting favours a variety of grassland settings,

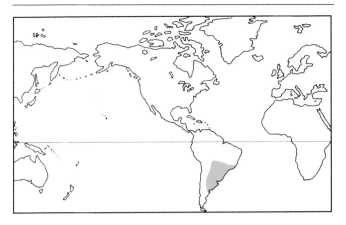

including prairies, hayfields, pastures and, more rarely, cultivated fields. Further north, found in clearings in spruce forests. On passage and in winter seen in a variety of short grass habitats. Generally found singly or in small groups.

Food Insects, mainly grasshoppers, crickets and weevils, also seeds and spilled wheat in the autumn.

Range Breeds in interior of North America from north-west Alaska south and east across western Canada and the central and eastern USA to Virginia and Maryland. Winters on the pampas of southern Brazil and Argentina, and beyond to the Rio Negro.

Movements It is a vagrant to western Europe and there have been 39 recorded sightings in Britain up to 1986, 24 of them since 1958.

RECORD OF SIGHTINGS			
Date _____		Date _____	
Place _____		Place _____	
Male(s) _____ Female(s) _____		Male(s) _____ Female(s) _____	
Immature ____ Eclipse _____		Immature ____ Eclipse _____	
Behaviour Notes			

Marsh Sandpiper
Tringa stagnatilis 22–25cm

Identification Slightly larger than a Wood Sandpiper, it more
closely resembles the larger Greenshank in its plumage patterns.
However, the disproportionately long, greenish legs and fine,
needle-like bill, combined with a rather small, ping-pong ball-like
head, long neck and slim body should preclude any confusion with
the latter species. In the breeding season the Marsh Sandpiper
acquires darker underparts, with wing and scapulars showing
irregular greyish-buff or fawn edgings to the feathers. The breast
develops dark spots, with greyish chevron markings at the sides and
down the flanks. The legs often turn a slightly brighter yellowish-
green colour. Juvenile resembles non-breeding adult but upperparts
are generally browner. In flight a white rump is revealed, extending
to a point in the centre of the back. This contrasts with the dark
wings and mantle. The long legs trail behind a slightly barred tail.
Voice In flight usually utters a 'teloo-tee-oo-tee-oo' like a faint,
higher-pitched Greenshank.
Habitat In breeding season river valleys and freshwater marshes.
In winter the margins of inland lakes, plus smaller creeks, lagoons
and estuaries on the coast.
Food Mainly insect larvae, water and terrestrial beetles, molluscs,
crustaceans and amphipods.
Range Generally extends from Austria eastwards through the

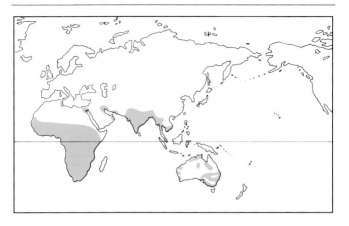

warmer mid-latitudes to northern Mongolia.

Movements Birds leave nesting grounds from late July onwards, moving on a broad front with few stops. They reach their wintering grounds in Africa, Madagascar, south and east Asia and, more sparsely, Australasia, by late August, early September. There appears to be a north-east to south-west element during autumn passage across North Africa and the Sahara and it is probably offshoots from this movement that are seen as vagrants in western Europe each year. Prior to 1976 an extremely rare visitor to Britain, with only 20 known records. Since 1976 it has been noted annually, with as many as eleven individuals during 1984. In recent years, breeding has been confirmed in Finland.

RECORD OF SIGHTINGS	
Date _____	Date _____
Place _____	Place _____
Male(s) _____ Female(s) _____	Male(s) _____ Female(s) _____
Immature ____ Eclipse _____	Immature ____ Eclipse _____
Behaviour Notes	

Greater Yellowlegs
Tringa melanoleuca   32–38cm

Identification A large, robust version of the commoner Lesser
Yellowlegs, the upperparts are generally dark brown, with various
lighter markings, including many small white flecks. The
underparts are white, streaked dark on the front and breast, with
barring on the sides. The bright yellow legs, which give the bird its
name, are brighter than Lesser Yellowlegs, while the bill is long
and slightly upcurved. The ratio of head to bill is a useful guide to
identification, the Greater Yellowleg's bill being one and a half
times as long as the head and somewhat broader at the base. In
flight there is a square white rump. The sexes are similar.
Voice Flight call is 'chu, chu, chu, chu'.
Habitat In breeding season open areas among tall woodland with
sparse undergrowth, interspersed with marshy pools. At other times
tidal beaches, mudflats, lagoons, flooded fields and similar watery
locations.

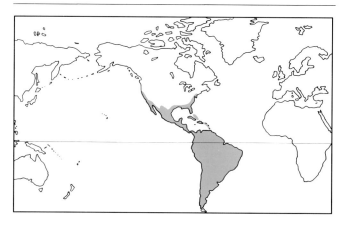

Food Worms, insect larvae, crustaceans, snails and, at times, grasshoppers.

Range Breeds in southern Alaska through British Columbia eastwards to Newfoundland and extending northwards to sub-Arctic tundra. Some winter in the southern states of the USA, but most move to the West Indies and South America. Stragglers have been drifted eastwards to Baffin Island, Greenland and to Britain.

Movements Birds reach the breeding grounds by the middle of May. After nesting, some birds are on their way south again at the end of July. Throughout August it is in full swing. By mid-October most birds have cleared the USA. A true rarity in Britain, making less than annual appearances. From 1977 to 1986, it has occurred in only four years.

RECORD OF SIGHTINGS	
Date _____	Date _____
Place _____	Place _____
Male(s) _____ Female(s) _____	Male(s) _____ Female(s) _____
Immature _____ Eclipse _____	Immature _____ Eclipse _____
Behaviour Notes	

Lesser Yellowlegs
Tringa flavipes   24–28cm

Identification A medium-sized, slender, almost dainty-looking bird, with long bright yellow legs. It is dark brown on the back and coverts, which are spotted and edged with white. The head, neck and upper breast are white and heavily streaked with grey, while the rest of the underparts are white and clean. In flight a square white rump is the most obvious feature, with disproportionately long wings, a grey and white barred tail and projecting legs. On its own it is a very confiding and approachable bird, nervously bobbing its head and tail. The long, slender bill is a major difference from the Greater Yellowlegs.

Voice A loud piercing 'kip, kip' on breeding grounds. Has a 'tew-tew' flight call.

Habitat For nesting chooses either hilly or flattish ground in the northern forest zone among trees with little undergrowth, wherever marshes and muskegs are close at hand. At other times coastal beaches, mudflats, brackish lagoons, freshwater lakes and pools; seems especially fond of flooded fields.

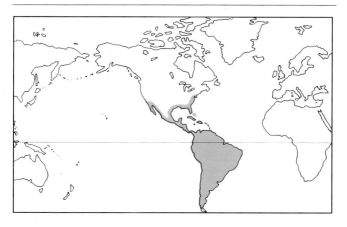

Food Crustaceans, small fish, insects and their larvae, and small aquatic life.

Range Nests in north central Alaska and adjacent Canadian provinces, including the Yukon, stretching southwards through the prairies and eastward to northern Ontario and western Quebec. Winters in the West Indies, Chile and Argentina. A vagrant to Europe.

Movements The autumn return is concentrated along the Atlantic seaboard when cyclonic weather conditions wind-drift some of these birds to Europe and Britain. Has been recorded in the British Isles on at least 190 occasions and is the sixth most numerous near-Arctic wader to reach the British side of the Atlantic.

RECORD OF SIGHTINGS	
Date _____	Date _____
Place _____	Place _____
Male(s) _____ Female(s) _____	Male(s) _____ Female(s) _____
Immature ____ Eclipse _____	Immature ____ Eclipse _____
Behaviour Notes	

Solitary Sandpiper
Tringa solitaria   18–21cm

Identification A medium-sized wader, with bill and legs neither exceptionally short nor long. The adult has blackish-brown upperparts, slightly paler and more olive on the head and neck, and finely speckled with white and buff. The breast is greyish-white and heavily streaked with dark brown, the streaking extending to the flanks; the rest of the underparts are white. In non-breeding plumage is a little paler and greyer with rather less spotting, while the juvenile is similar to the summer adult, but a bit browner with buffer spotting. In all plumages the legs are grey-green and the bill blackish with an olive base. There is a prominent white eye-ring and a short stripe extending from the bill to the eye. In flight shows dark wings and a dark rump and tail. There is some barring to the sides of the tail.

Voice Normally a thin, weak 'pip' or 'pip-pip'. In full flight utters a 'pleet-weet-weet' sharper than Spotted Sandpiper.

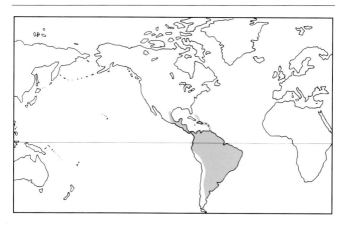

Habitat In breeding season found in open coniferous forest in the vicinity of water. On passage can turn up beside any patch of water. In winter frequents rivers and edges of lakes and ponds, also coastal mangroves.

Food Insects, small crustaceans, spiders and small frogs.

Range Breeds from Alaska across Canada to Labrador, north to the tree-line and south to a line from central British Columbia to central Ontario.

Movements It is a vagrant to western Europe, with 24 sightings in Britain. There have only been seven records between 1977 and 1986. The majority of records have been in the south-west, particularly the Isles of Scilly.

RECORD OF SIGHTINGS	
Date _____	Date _____
Place _____	Place _____
Male(s) _____ Female(s) _____	Male(s) _____ Female(s) _____
Immature _____ Eclipse _____	Immature _____ Eclipse _____
Behaviour Notes	

Spotted Sandpiper
Actitus macularia   18–20cm

Identification In breeding plumage, with its spotted underparts, this small sandpiper is most distinctive. Also noticeable are the numerous black cross-bars on the olive brown upperparts. There is a whitish supercilium and the base of the shortish bill is pinkish. The legs are orange-yellow or pinkish. In winter it shows relatively pale unmarked olive or grey-brown upperparts, with all-white underparts and yellowish legs. There is a dark patch at the side of the neck, and between this and the bend of the wing, a very distinctive white shoulder mark. Its teetering, bobbing gait is most characteristic, as is its flight, which is low over the water, with flickering wingbeats interspersed with frequent glides. There are short narrow wing bars, and the tail and rump are unmarked.
Voice In flight gives a shrill 'peet-weet' or a 'weet-weet-weet'. Sometimes a quiet 'pit' note is uttered.
Habitat Most waterside conditions from sea level to the tree-line suit it for nesting, though it sometimes nests well away from water. Quite often chooses farmland or pastures. At other times shores of

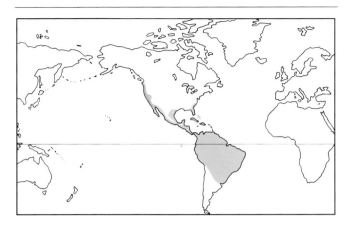

lakes, creeks, lagoons, flooded fields and marshy areas. Shuns the open shore.

Food Insects and a range of freshwater invertebrates.

Range Breeds across North America from Alaska to Newfoundland, and south to southern California, North Carolina and Maryland. Winters in west, from British Columbia southwards to Peru, and east, from the Carolinas to Argentina. A vagrant to eastern Siberia, Tristan da Cunha and Marshall Islands in the central Pacific, as well as to western Europe.

Movements In Britain 83 have been recorded, almost all since the late 1960s, in spring, summer and autumn, many of which have been summer-plumaged adults. A pair attempted to nest in Scotland in 1975 and birds have overwintered on five occasions.

RECORD OF SIGHTINGS

Date _____	Date _____
Place _____	Place _____
Male(s) _____ Female(s) _____	Male(s) _____ Female(s) _____
Immature _____ Eclipse _____	Immature _____ Eclipse _____

Behaviour Notes

Terek Sandpiper
Xenus cinereus   22–25cm

Identification Gives the impression of a medium-large, pale, long-billed sandpiper. Superficially similar to Common Sandpiper, but has a bulky body with a short thick neck, and a rather angular head with a high forehead. Most notable is the long, gently upcurved bill which, with the generally pale grey upperparts, white underparts and short yellowish legs, make identification certain. In breeding plumage is grey above, marked with irregular dark line along the scapulars, which is most prominent head-on or rear-on. The underparts are white, with a paler grey wash on the sides of the breast, across which a band of fine streaks may join the centre. The dark scapular line is lost in winter. The juvenile is browner, with fine buff scales on the upperparts; it also has black scapular lines. The bill is black, often with a yellowish base in winter, and juvenile plumage. In flight shows a narrow, white trailing edge to the inner wings. The rump and tail are grey.

Voice In flight utters a tittering whistle; on the ground gives a Redshank-like 'du-du-du' or 'du-du', as well as a piping 'wit-e-wit' and 'too-li'.

Habitat For breeding prefers gently-flowing fresh water with open, soft, moist ground and dense patches of vegetation. In winter haunts the coast, favouring muddy beaches, mangrove creeks and coral.

Food Aquatic insects and marine invertebrates. Seeds are taken on the breeding grounds.

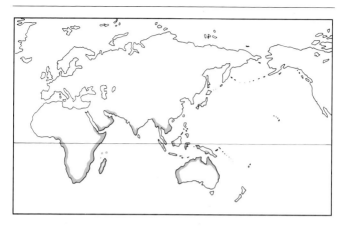

Range Named after the Terek river, breeds in an area of northern Europe and Asia that extends from the Baltic States eastward to eastern Siberia. There is a recently established small population around Kiev on the Baltic coast of Finland. Has bred once in Norway. Winters along the coasts of southern and eastern Africa and the shores of the Indian Ocean. Is most abundant in India, south-east Asia, Indonesia and northern Australia.

Movements In spring birds head north to reach breeding grounds from mid-May to early June. Often nesting adults head south in the first half of July, but juveniles do not follow until August or September. It is rare in western Europe and there are only 28 records of this species in Britain, but has been more regular since the mid-1970s.

RECORD OF SIGHTINGS	
Date _____	Date _____
Place _____	Place _____
Male(s) _____ Female(s) _____	Male(s) _____ Female(s) _____
Immature _____ Eclipse _____	Immature _____ Eclipse _____
Behaviour Notes	

Wilson's Phalarope

Phalaropus tricolor   22–24cm

Identification Largest of the phalaropes, it shows a disproportionately bulky body, a long slender neck and small rounded head. Additionally, the shortish legs are placed well back on its body, giving a top-heavy, pot-bellied look. As with other phalaropes, the female is more brightly coloured and in breeding plumage shows a strikingly pronounced thick, black patch extending from the base of her bill through the face, then down the side of the neck, separating the bright white throat, chestnut foreneck and upper breast from the pearl-grey crown, hindneck and nape. In winter the sexes are alike, being pale grey-brown above and white below. Sometimes there is a dark mark through the eye. The black bill is long and needle-fine, the legs are yellowish (black in summer plumage). In flight shows dark wings and white rump. When feeding in shallow water, 'spins' characteristically. However, less aquatic than other phalaropes and more frequently feeds along water's edge, running on mud with a lurching gait.

Voice A nasal grunting 'aangh'. Also has a flight call 'chu'.

Habitat In breeding season found on prairie wetland meadows, at other times inland lakes and pools, and on migration any waterside situation.

Food Comprises a varied diet of spiders, beetles, crustaceans,

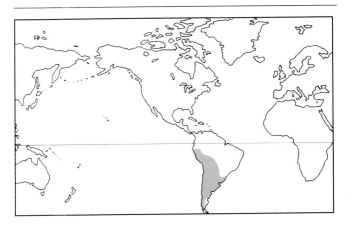

insects and their larvae. Aquatic plant seeds are also taken.

Range As a breeding species, presently found in north-west, north central and middle USA and Canada, covering at least 16 states from Manitoba south to central California, stretching to Kansas, then north-east to the Great Lakes. In Canada its expanding range now extends from British Columbia to Ontario. Winters entirely on inland lakes and pools of the Argentinian and Chilean pampas, and also at high-altitude lakes in Peru.

Movements Not recorded in the British Isles until 1954, when one was seen in Fife. Since 1961 the species has occurred annually and is now the fifth most numerous transatlantic wader reaching Britain and Ireland.

RECORD OF SIGHTINGS	
Date _____	Date _____
Place _____	Place _____
Male(s) _____ Female(s) _____	Male(s) _____ Female(s) _____
Immature _____ Eclipse _____	Immature _____ Eclipse _____
Behaviour Notes	

Appendix

The following is a list of species not included in the main text, but which have been recorded either regularly or intermittently in Europe.

Greater Sand Plover
Charadrius leschenaultii
OTHER NAMES Large Sand Dotterel, Large Sand Plover, Geoffrey's Plover

Breeds from southern USSR, east to Mongolia; winters on coasts from East Africa to Australia. Passage migrant and vagrant to many parts of the world. More prone to westward vagrancy than the Lesser Sand Plover, with records across Europe to France and Scandinavia. Seven records for the British Isles.

Sharp-tailed Sandpiper
Calidris acuminata
OTHER NAME Siberian Pectoral Sandpiper

Breeds in north Siberia; winters in Australasia. Regular passage migrant to west Alaska. A vagrant to Canada and the USA (mostly on Pacific coast), Scandinavia, France, the British Isles (19 records), and parts of Asia.

Sociable Plover
Chettusia gregaria
OTHER NAME Sociable Lapwing

Breeds in south-east USSR, and western central Asia; winters further south in Asia and Africa. Is strongly migratory, with westward vagrancy to most European countries, except Scandinavia. Recorded 29 times in the British Isles.

White-tailed Lapwing
Chettusia leucura
OTHER NAME White-tailed Plover

Breeding and wintering ranges similar to Sociable Plover, but also breeds in the Middle East. Less prone to westward vagrancy, but has occurred north to Finland and Sweden, and west to France and the British Isles, with four records in the latter country.

Red-necked Stint
Calidris ruficollis

OTHER NAMES Rufous-necked Stint, Rufous-necked Sandpiper
Breeds in north and north-east Siberia and occasionally west Alaska; winters in south-east Asia and Australasia. In North America a vagrant to south-east Alaska, British Columbia, Oregon, California, the Atlantic coast of the USA, and Bermuda. In Europe a vagrant to west USSR, and both East and West Germany; a 1986 record from Britain is still under consideration.

Long-toed Stint
Calidris subminuta

Breeds in Siberia; winters in south-east Asia, the Philippines and Australasia. A vagrant to Sweden, British Isles (one record), west Aleutians, west Alaska, and Oregon, plus one or two places in East Africa and the Indian Ocean.

Caspian Plover
Charadrius asiaticus

Breeds south-east USSR, and west central Asia; winters in South and East Africa. Vagrant south-eastwards to Australia and westwards across Europe to Italy, Malta, France and Norway. One British record in 1890.

Little Whimbrel
Numenius minutus

OTHER NAME Little Curlew
Rare breeder in central and north-east Siberia; winters in Australasia. Vagrant to British Isles (two records), Norway, California, and a few other scattered areas outside Europe and North America.

Eskimo Curlew
Numenius borealis

This tiny curlew is teetering on the brink of extinction and only a few pairs may still exist, breeding in one part of northern Canada. There are several records of this bird in Britain during the latter half of the nineteenth century.

Index

Acknowledgements

I am grateful to the many photographers for the excellence of their illustrations. Their names are listed here against the page number where their photographs appear.

Front Cover top: E. Soothill   bottom: D. K. Richards
Title Page C. Smith

6 A. J. Bond	**72** R. Glover
8 R. T. Mills	**74** M. C. Wilkes
10 S. C. Brown	**76** C. Greaves
12 M. C. Wilkes	**78** A. T. Moffett
13 R. T. Mills	**80** M. C. Wilkes
14 R. Glover	**82** M. C. Wilkes
16 M. C. Wilkes	**84** W. Lankinen
18 J. Lawton Roberts	**86** R. Glover
20 B. L. Sage	**88** S. P. Myers/Vireo
22 Larking and Powell	**90** M. C. Wilkes
24 M. C. Wilkes	**91** M. C. Wilkes
26 R. Maier	**92** T. Leach
28 J. L. Roberts	**94** W. Lankinen
30 D. S. Whitaker	**96** T. Leach
32 A. W. M. Aitchison	**98** R. P. Tipper
34 R. Glover	**100** W. Lankinen
36 M. C. Wilkes	**102** Dr. J. Davies
38 R. Glover	**104** M. C. Wilkes
40 M. C. Wilkes	**106** D. M. Cotteridge
42 P. Doherty	**108** R. T. Mills
44 C. Greaves	**110** P. Doherty
46 R. T. Mills	**112** W. Lankinen
48 C. Greaves	**114** J. B. & S. Bottomley
50 H. A. Hems	**116** W. Lankinen
52 M. C. Wilkes	**118** J. B. & S. Bottomley
54 M. C. Wilkes	**120** W. Lankinen
56 C. Greaves	**122** G. R. Jones
58 M. C. Wilkes	**124** M. C. Wilkes
60 B. S. Barnacel	**126** M. C. Wilkes
62 B. Speake	**128** W. Lankinen
64 R. T. Mills	**130** G. Langsbury
66 R. Glover	**132** W. Lankinen
68 S. & B. Craig	**134** C. Greaves
70 A. J. Bond	**136** S. B. & S. Bottomley

Title Page Waders flock over the Dee Estuary
Page 14 Dunlin and Grey Plover roosting along beach
Page 92 Mixed waders along a Florida shoreline in spring

RSNC

The Royal Society for Nature Conservation is pleased to endorse these excellent, fully illustrated pocket guide books which provide invaluable information on the wildlife of Britain and Northern Europe. Royalties from each book sold will go to help the RSNC's network of 48 Wildlife Trusts and over 50 Urban Wildlife Groups, all working to protect rare and endangered wildlife and threatened habitats. The RSNC and the Wildlife Trusts have a combined membership of 184,000 and look after over 1,800 nature reserves. If you would like to find out more, please contact the RSNC, The Green, Nettleham, Lincoln, LN2 2NR, Telephone 0522 752326.